NATIONAL QUALIFICATIC

General MATHEMATICS
Model Papers

The National Qualifications' Examination Questions and the Scottish Certificate of Education Examination Questions are reprinted by special permission of
THE SCOTTISH QUALIFICATIONS AUTHORITY

> The model papers printed in this publication do not emanate from the S.Q.A. They are based on past examination questions and reflect in the opinion of the author what might be expected in the General Mathematics examination.

ISBN 0 7169 9337 6
© *Robert Gibson & Sons, Glasgow, Ltd.,* 2000

ROBERT GIBSON · Publisher
17 Fitzroy Place, Glasgow, G3 7SF.

FORMULAE LIST

Circumference of a circle: $C = \pi d$
Area of a circle: $A = \pi r^2$
Curved surface area of a cylinder: $A = 2\pi r h$
Volume of a cylinder: $V = \pi r^2 h$
Volume of a triangular prism: $V = Ah$

Theorem of Pythagoras:

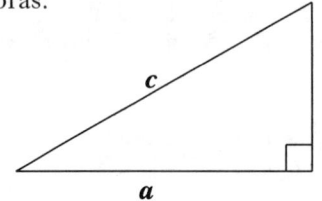

$$a^2 + b^2 = c^2$$

Trigonometric ratios in a right angled triangle:

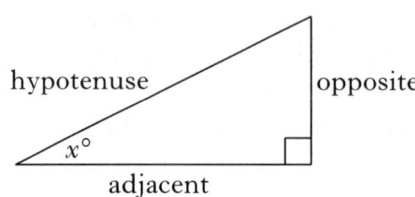

$$\tan x° = \frac{\text{opposite}}{\text{adjacent}}$$

$$\sin x° = \frac{\text{opposite}}{\text{hypotenuse}}$$

$$\cos x° = \frac{\text{adjacent}}{\text{hypotenuse}}$$

Gradient:

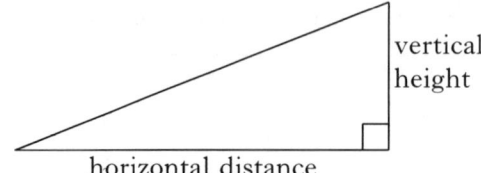

$$\text{Gradient} = \frac{\text{vertical height}}{\text{horizontal distance}}$$

COPYING PROHIBITED

Note: This publication is **NOT** licensed for copying under the Copyright Licensing Agency's Scheme, to which Robert Gibson & Sons are not party.

All rights reserved. No part of this publication may be reproduced; stored in a retrieval system; or transmitted in any form or by any means — electronic, mechanical, photocopying, or otherwise — without prior permission of the publisher Robert Gibson & Sons, Ltd., 17 Fitzroy Place, Glasgow, G3 7SF.

NATIONAL QUALIFICATIONS

MATHEMATICS

Standard Grade — GENERAL LEVEL

INSTRUCTIONS TO CANDIDATES

Paper 1
(Non-calculator)
Time: 35 minutes

1 **Calculators may NOT be used in this paper.**

2 Answer as many questions as you can.

3 Write your working and answers in the spaces provided. Additional space is provided at the end of this question-answer book for use if required. If you use this space, write clearly the number of the question involved.

4 Full credit will be given only where the solution contains appropriate working.

5 Before leaving the examination room you must give this book to the invigilator. If you do not, you may lose all the marks for this paper.

Paper 2
Time: 55 minutes

1 **Calculators may be used in this paper.**

2 Answer as many questions as you can.

3 Write your working and answers in the spaces provided. Additional space is provided at the end of this question-answer book for use if required. If you use this space, write clearly the number of the question involved.

4 Full credit will be given only where the solution contains appropriate working.

5 Before leaving the examination room you must give this book to the invigilator. If you do not, you may lose all the marks for this paper.

NATIONAL
QUALIFICATIONS
MODEL PAPER A

MATHEMATICS
STANDARD GRADE
General Level
Paper 1
(Non-calculator)

	KU	RE

1. Carry out the following calculations
    (a) 70% of £26 — **2**
    (b) 5 + 11·31 − 12·8 — **1**
    (c) 0·16 × 60 — **1**
    (d) 53·15 ÷ 5. — **1**

2. Michael's monthly salary is £720.

    He spends $\frac{1}{5}$ of this on his mortgage, $\frac{3}{20}$ on his car and $\frac{1}{10}$ on insurance.

    He uses the remainder for his household expenses.

    How much money does he spend on his car each month? — **2**

3. The brightest star in the sky has a diameter of 2·33 million kilometres.

    (a) Write 2·33 million in figures. — **1**

    (b) Write 2·33 million in scientific notation. — **1**

4. The table shows the average winter temperatures in four cities.

	London	New York	Rome	Moscow
Average winter temperature	3 °C	−2 °C	6 °C	−8 °C

    (a) What is the difference between the average winter temperatures in London and Moscow? — **2**

    (b) One winter's day, the temperature in New York was 7 degrees below average.
    What was the temperature that day? — **1**

4

5. (a) Draw the next T-shape in this sequence.

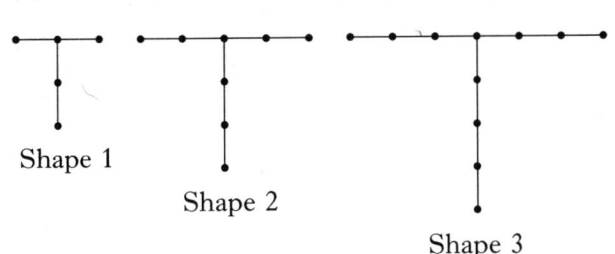

Shape 1

Shape 2

Shape 3

Shape 4

(b) Complete the following table.

Shape Number (s)	1	2	3	4	5		16
Number of dots (d)	5		11				

(c) Write down a formula for the number of dots (d) when you know the shape number (s).

6. New York time is 5 hours behind British time.

When it is 7 pm in Britain, it is 2 pm in New York.

(a) At 10 am Gordon, who is in New York, phones home to Britain. What time is it in Britain?

(b) Los Angeles time is 3 hours behind New York time.

From Los Angeles, Fiona needs to phone a colleague in Aberdeen before 6 pm, British time.

She makes the phone call at 9.30 am, Los Angeles time.

Does she meet the 6 pm deadline?

Give a reason for your answer.

7. (a) Solve **algebraically** the equation

$$4x - 5 = x + 22$$

(b) Factorise

$$8a - 12b.$$

8.

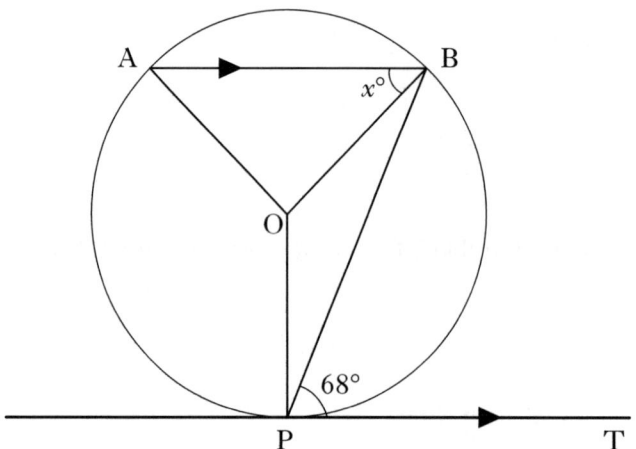

PT is a tangent to the circle, centre O.

PT is parallel to AB.

Angle BPT = 68°.

(a) What is the size of the angle BPO?

(b) Calculate the size of the angle marked $x°$.

9. Ticketmasters Call Centre can handle 240 calls for concert tickets every 2 hours.

How many calls can they handle in 45 minutes?

PAPER 2

Calculators may be used in this paper.

1. Bryony is taking part in a dance competition.

   The two judges, Judge A and Judge B, were scoring the competitors. Each judge awarded points out of 50.

   The scattergraph below shows the marks for the six competitors who have already taken part in the competition.

   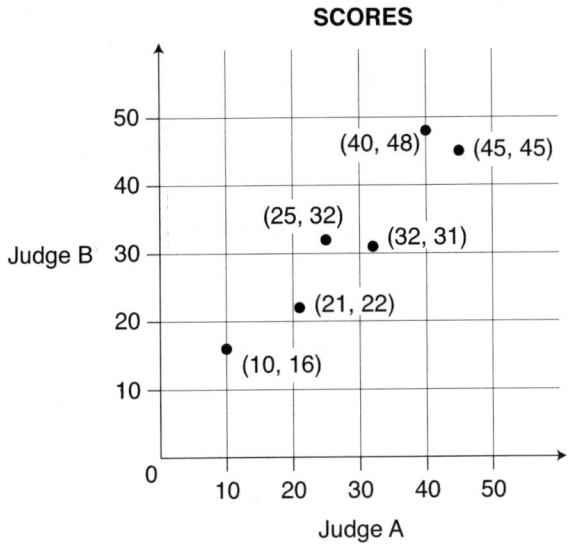

   (a) Bryony was awarded a score of 35 by Judge A and 38 by Judge B.

   Mark Bryony's score with an X on the scattergraph.

   (b) Draw a line of best fit on the scattergraph.

   (c) Siobhan was awarded a score of 30 by Judge A.

   From your scattergraph estimate the score that Judge B should award Siobhan.

2. A house loses heat through its roof, walls, windows and doors.

In the Grant family's bungalow 23% of its heat loss is through the roof.

The **total** heat loss from the house costs the Grant family £650 each year.

(a) Calculate the annual cost of the heat loss through the roof.

(b) If the Grant family insulate their loft, the heat lost through the roof will be reduced by two thirds.

How much money will they save each year if they insulate their loft?

(c) It will cost the Grants £750 to insulate their loft.

How long will it take them to recover their expenditure on the insulation?

3. The diagram below shows a triangular flag which is 28 centimetres across and 46 centimetres long.

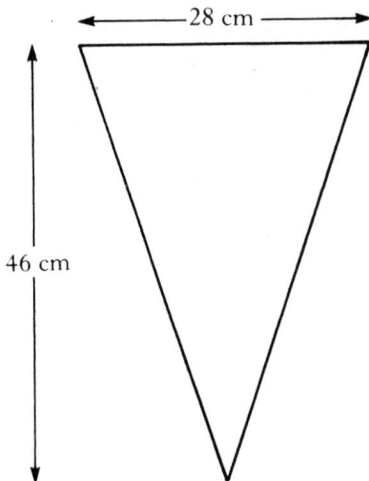

Calculate the area of the flag.

Model Paper A

4. To raise money for its funds, a school organises a competition.

In this competition, each person selects **10** football teams.

Points are awarded as follows.

	Points
Win	3
Score Draw	2
No-Score Draw	1
Loss	0

PRIZES ARE AWARDED FOR 27 POINTS OR MORE

One way of winning a prize is shown in the table below.

Number of teams getting 3 points	Number of teams getting 2 points	Number of teams getting 1 point	Number of teams getting 0 points	Total number of points
9	0	1	0	28
10	0	0	0	30
9	1	0	0	29
9	0	0	1	27
8	2	0	0	28
8	1	1	0	27
7	3	0	0	27

Complete the table to show all the different ways of winning a prize.

5. (a) Complete the table below for $y = 3x + 1$.

x	−3	0	3
y			

(b) Using the table in part (a), draw the graph of the line $y = 3x + 1$ on the grid below.

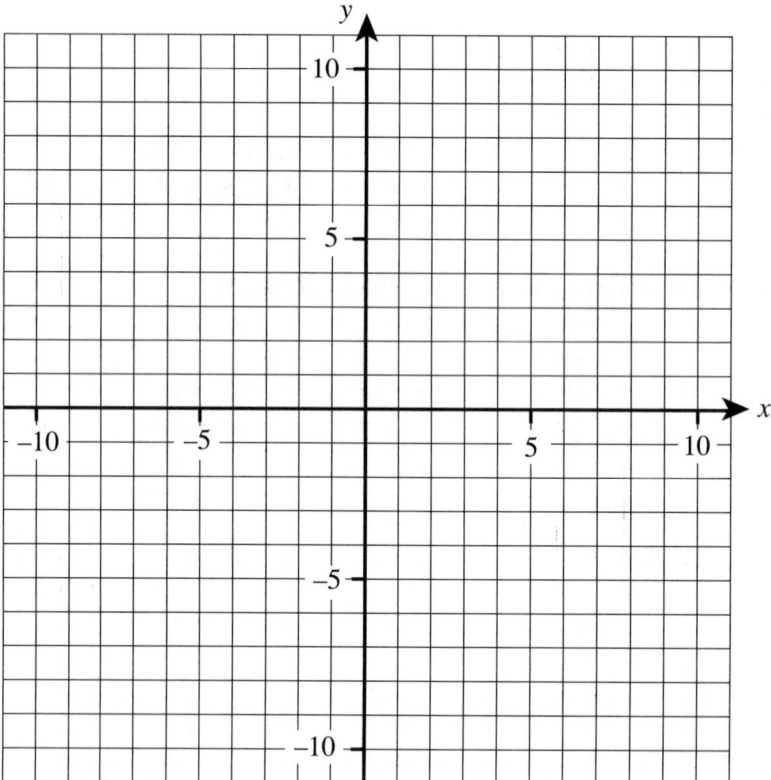

6. The number of people visiting a rural shop over a number of days was recorded on a frequency table.

No. of people	Frequency	No. of people × frequency
10	8	80
11	5	55
12	10	120
13	9	117
14	8	
	40	

(a) Complete the table and calculate the mean.

(b) What was the range of the distribution?

7. Brigton and Farlap are two small towns 6 kilometres apart.
A by-pass is being built to reduce the traffic passing through the two towns, as shown in the diagram.

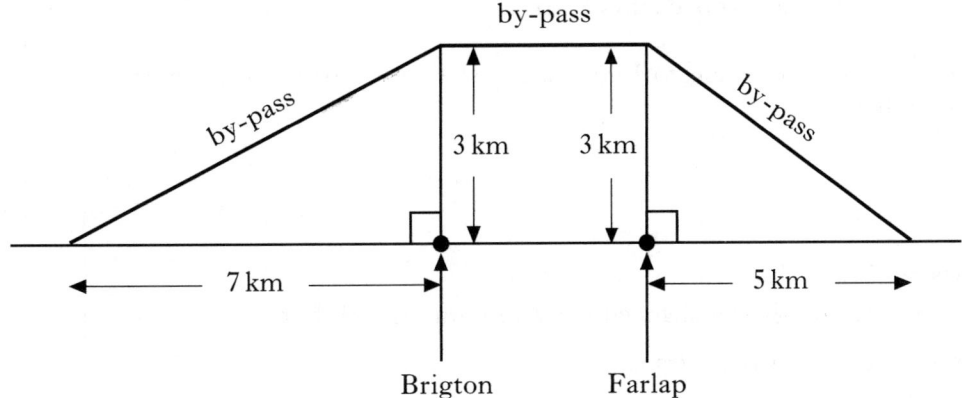

Calculate the total length of the by-pass.

8. The sketch below shows the journey of a ship from a harbour.

The ship leaves the harbour and sails a distance of 30 kilometres on a bearing of 025° and then sails for 50 kilometres on a bearing of 070°.

(a) Make a scale drawing of the ship's course.

 Use the scale **1 cm represents 5 km**.

(b) Use your scale drawing to find the actual distance of the ship from the harbour.

9. Sunni visited France last year for seven days.
Before going on holiday she changed her £150 into French francs.

The rate of exchange was 8·5 francs to the £.

On holiday she spent 100 francs each day.

When she returned home she changed the remaining francs back into pounds.

The rate of exchange was 9·2 francs to the £.

She was charged £4 for changing the francs back into pounds.

How much did Sunni receive?

10. The angle of elevation from the ground to the top of a block of flats is 48°. The angle is measured at a point 75 metres from the flats as shown in the diagram below.

Calculate the height, h metres, of the block of flats, correct to 1 decimal place.

11.

A milk carton is in the shape of a cuboid with a square base.

The sides of the base are 8 centimetres long.

(a) The volume of the carton is 1280 cubic centimetres.

What is the height of the carton?

(b) A second cuboid carton, which also has a square base, holds 1·75 litres of milk.

The height of this carton is 25 cm.

Find the length of the base.

12. A pattern of circular discs of **diameter 6 centimetres** is to be cut from a square sheet of plastic.

The diagram below shows part of this sheet.

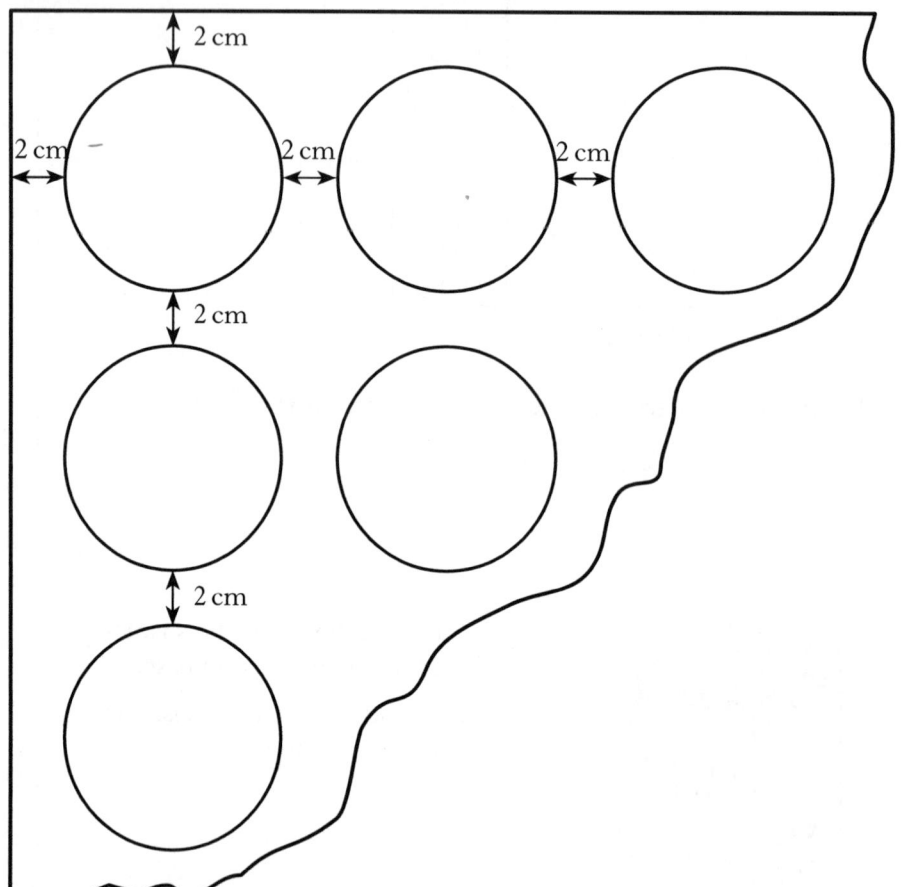

(a) How many circular discs could be cut from a square sheet of plastic of side 50 centimetres?

(b) Find the area of plastic remaining after the discs have been cut from the square sheet.

[END OF QUESTION PAPER]

NATIONAL
QUALIFICATIONS
MODEL PAPER B

MATHEMATICS
STANDARD GRADE
General Level
Paper 1
(Non-calculator)

	KU	RE

1. Carry out the following calculations

    (*a*) 15% of 200 m   2

    (*b*) 13·2 − 4·9 + 0·17   1

    (*c*) 2·47 × 5   1

    (*d*) 24·64 ÷ 7.   1

2. The average mass of a grain of pollen is $2\cdot3 \times 10^{-5}$ grams.
Write this number out in full.   2

3. The temperature recorded at 6 am in Aviemore is shown on the diagram below.

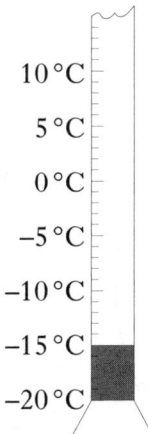

(*a*) By 9 am, the temperature had risen to −7 °C.

    By how many degrees had the temperature risen?   1

(*b*) By 2 pm, the temperature had risen by a further 9 degrees.

    What was the temperature at 2 pm?   1

4. The graph shows some information about two boys, Alexander and Darren.

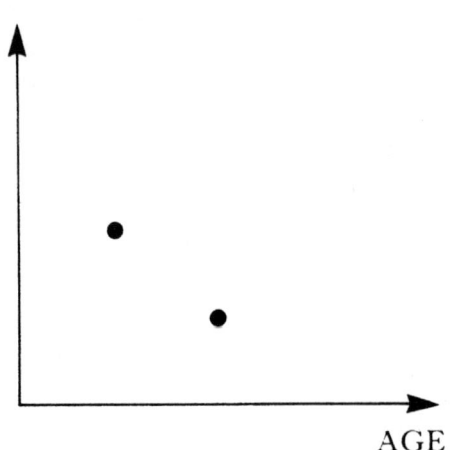

Alexander is older than Darren.

(a) Label the dots on the graph with the names of the two boys.

(b) What else does the graph tell you about the boys?

(c) Claire is the same age as Darren and is taller than both boys.

Show this information by marking a dot on the graph above.

5.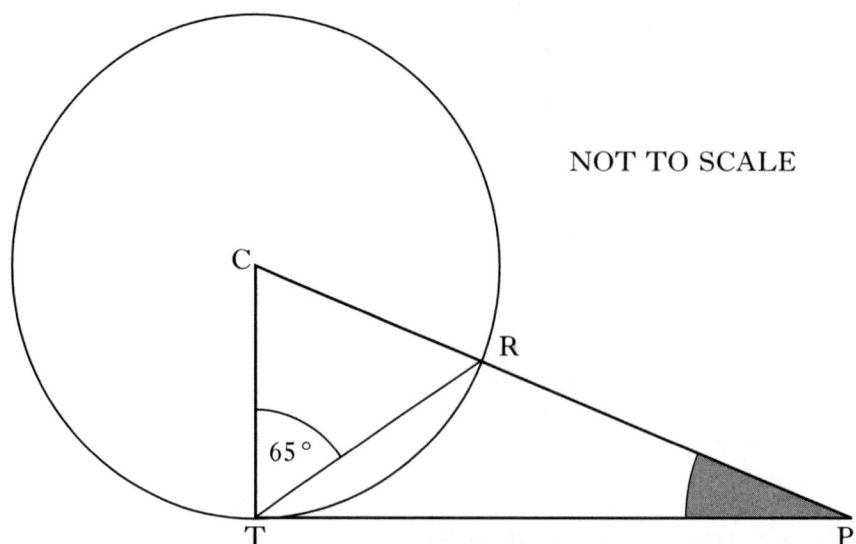

The diagram shows a circle with centre C.
PT is a tangent to the circle at the point T.
Angle CTR is 65°.

(a) Explain why angle CRT is also 65°.

(b) Calculate the size of the shaded angle.

6. The sides of a bridge are constructed by joining sections.

The sections are made of steel girders.

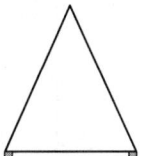
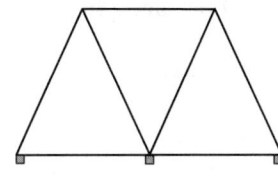
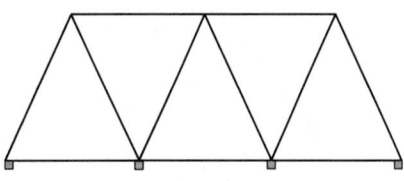

1 section
3 girders

2 sections
7 girders

3 sections

(a) Complete the table below.

Number of sections (s)	1	2	3	4		10
Number of girders (g)	3	7				

(b) Write down a formula for the number of girders, g, when you know the number of sections, s.

7. (a) Multiply out the brackets and simplify

$$2a + 3(4a - 5).$$

(b) Solve **algebraically** the equation

$$4x - 3 = x + 5.$$

8.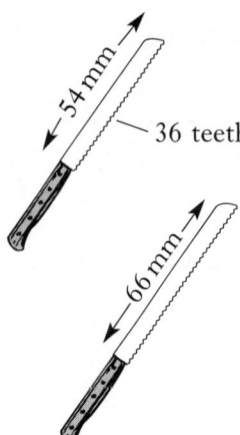

The blade of a knife is 54 millimetres long.

The blade has 36 teeth.

The blade of a larger knife is 66 millimetres long.

The ratio $\dfrac{\text{number of teeth}}{\text{length of blade}}$ is the same for both knives.

How many teeth does the larger knife have?

9. A 5-sided spinner has the numbers 1 to 5 marked on its sides. It is equally likely to land on any side when spun.

When it is spun, what is the probability that it will land on a 3?

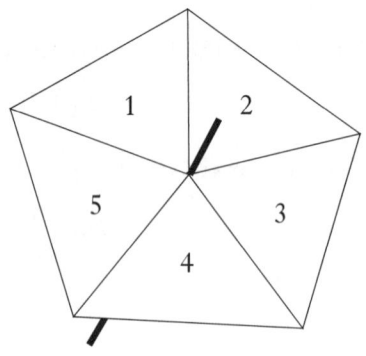

Model Paper B

PAPER 2

Calculators may be used in this paper.

		KU	RE

1. Here is part of a French Railway timetable for a high-speed train.

Distance from Paris (km)		
0	Paris	Depart 1649
512	Lyon	Depart 1900
617	Valence	Depart 1955
742	Avignon	Depart 2051
863	Marseille	Arrive 2144

(a) How many kilometres is it from Valence to Marseille?   1

(b) Calculate the journey time from Valence to Marseille.   2

(c) Find the speed of the train from Valence to Marseille.
Round your answer to the nearest kilometre per hour.   2

2. The marks for 20 pupils in class 1A in a test are displayed in the stem-and-leaf diagram below.

```
0 | 9
1 | 3 4 4
2 | 0 1 7 9 9      Key 2 / 0 means 20.
3 | 2 2 5 6 7 9
4 | 0 0 1 4 8
```

(a) How many pupils scored 32?   1

(b) What was the highest marked scored?   1

(c) What was the median mark?   2

3. The Computer Store buys this computer for £250 and sells it to make a profit of 40%.

(a) What is the selling price of this computer?

(b) The Computer Store adds 20% to the **selling price** when a customer buys the computer on hire purchase.

Hire purchase terms are a £30 deposit followed by 24 equal monthly payments.

Calculate the customer's monthly payment.

4. (a) On the grid below, plot the points A (−8, −3) and B (4, 6).

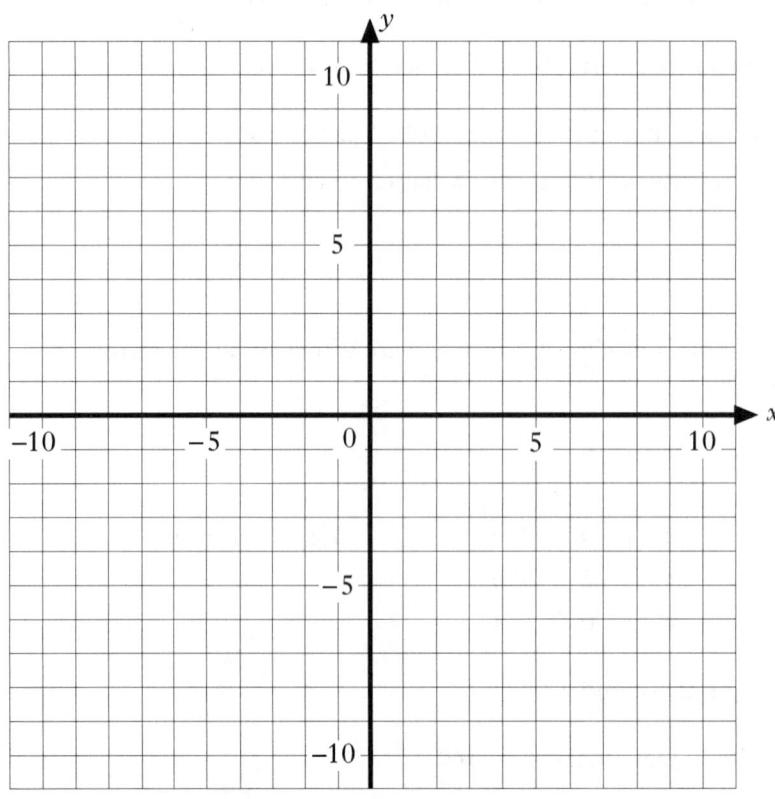

(b) Find the gradient of the line AB.

5. The lowest temperature (°C) was recorded each day for seven days during the winter on a remote Scottish island.

   The temperatures were:

   $$-2 \quad 1 \quad -4 \quad 0 \quad -7 \quad 3 \quad -5.$$

   Calculate the average temperature over the seven days.

6. Draw the image of the shape reflected in the line AB.

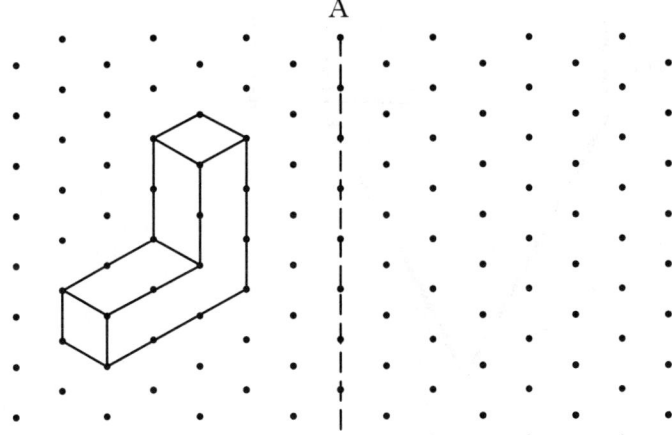

7. A banner is to be edged all round with gold braid.

The banner is in the shape of a rectangle with an isosceles triangle below it, as shown in the diagram.

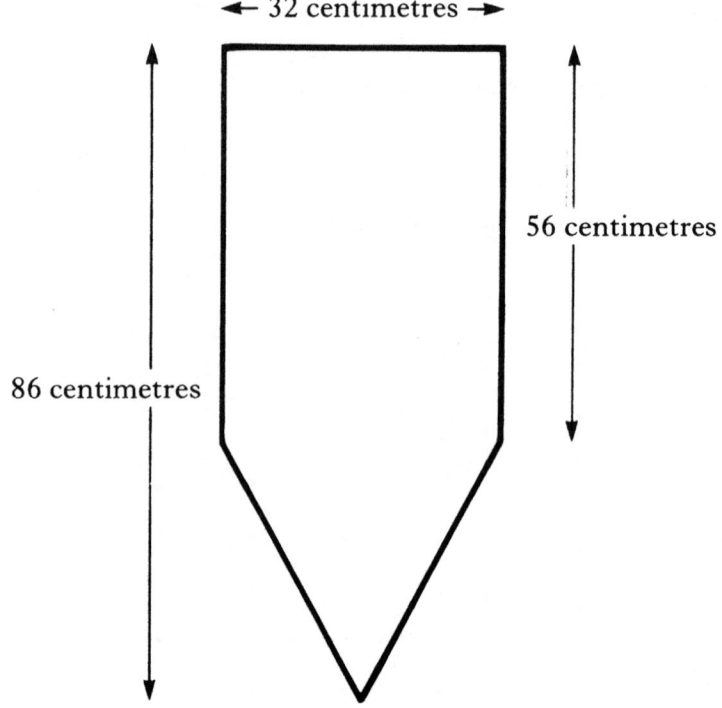

Calculate the total length of gold braid needed.

8. Mallaig and Lochboisdale are two small ports in the Northwest of Scotland.

The scale drawing shows the positions of Mallaig and Lochboisdale, which are 95 kilometres apart.

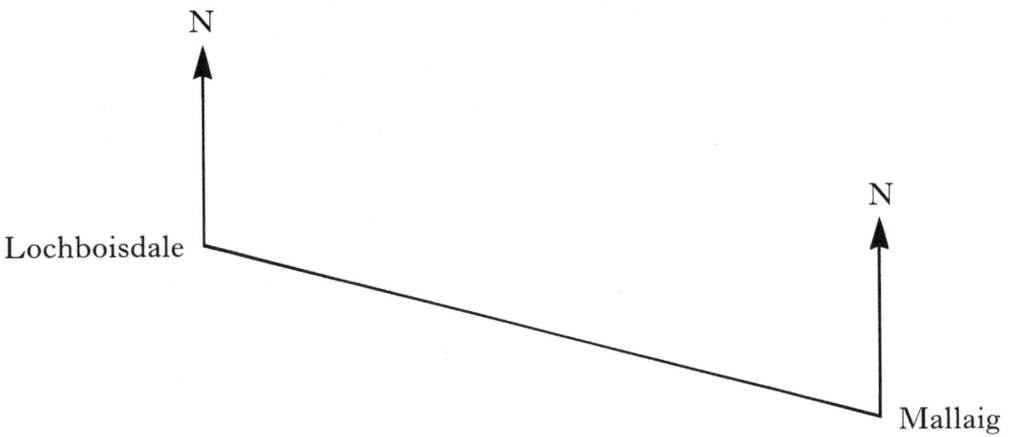

(a) Write down the scale of the drawing.

(b) A third port, Castlebay, is on a bearing of 210° from Lochboisdale and is due West of Mallaig.

Complete the scale drawing above to show the position of Castlebay.

(c) Use the scale drawing to find the distance in kilometres between Castlebay and Lochboisdale.

9. Chris needs to use a ladder to put up a television aerial on the wall of the house.

The ladder is 5 metres long and has to reach 4·8 metres up the wall.

For safety, the angle between the ladder and the ground should be between 71° and 76°.

The ground is horizontal.

Can Chris use this ladder safely?

You must give a reason for your answer.

10. A superstore has three kinds of paint.

£3·99   £4·99   £6·49

(a) Using the information shown above, explain why Coverite appears to give the best value for money.

(b) On the backs of the tins there is more information.

Using this additional information, decide which paint is the best value for money.

You must show all your working.

11. Mr and Mrs Campbell's children have had their photographs taken at school.

The photographs are available in the following packs.

> PACK A costs £8·00
> PACK B costs £6.50
> PACK C costs £5.50

Mr and Mrs Campbell want to buy 3 packs of photographs but decide to spend not more than £20 in total.

One way they could do this is to buy 1 of pack B and 2 of pack C which would cost a total of £17.50.

This is shown in the first row of the table below.

Number of Pack A	Number of Pack B	Number of Pack C
	1	2

Fill in the rest of the table to show all the different ways Mr and Mrs Campbell could buy 3 packs of photographs of their children.

12. A dairy produces a 500 gram pack of butter in the shape of a cylinder.

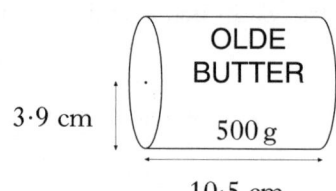

3·9 cm

10·5 cm

The radius of the circular end of the pack is 3·9 centimetres and the length of the pack is 10·5 centimetres.

(a) Calculate the volume of the pack of butter.

Give your answer to the nearest whole number.

The 500 gram pack is redesigned. It is now produced in the shape of a cuboid with a square end of side 6·5 centimetres.

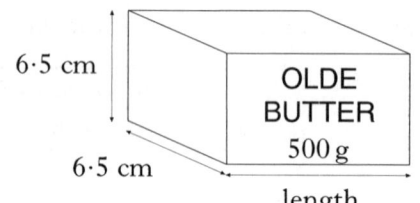

6·5 cm

6·5 cm

length

(b) Calculate the length of the redesigned pack of butter.

Give your answer correct to 1 decimal place.

[END OF QUESTION PAPER]

NATIONAL
QUALIFICATIONS
MODEL PAPER C

MATHEMATICS
STANDARD GRADE
General Level
Paper 1
(Non-calculator)

	KU	RE

1. Carry out the following calculations

(a) 75% of £300 — KU: 2

(b) 5·147 − 2·38 — KU: 1

(c) 0·013 × 300 — KU: 1

(d) 38·32 ÷ 4. — KU: 1

2. The table below appeared in a newspaper and shows when street lights should come on and go off.

Lighting-up Times			
London	4.43 pm	to	7.44 am
Bristol	4.52 pm	to	7.53 am
Birmingham	4.46 pm	to	7.54 am
Manchester	4.43 pm	to	8.00 am
Newcastle	4.35 pm	to	8.03 am
Glasgow	4.41 pm	to	8.17 am
Belfast	4.54 pm	to	8.18 am

(a) How long, in hours and minutes, were the street lights on in Glasgow? — KU: 2

(b) Was the time of year summer or winter?

You must give a reason for your answer. — RE: 2

KU	RE

3. The cost of hiring a Yellow Taxi consists of a basic charge plus a charge per kilometre.

The cost of journeys up to 10 kilometres is shown in the graph below.

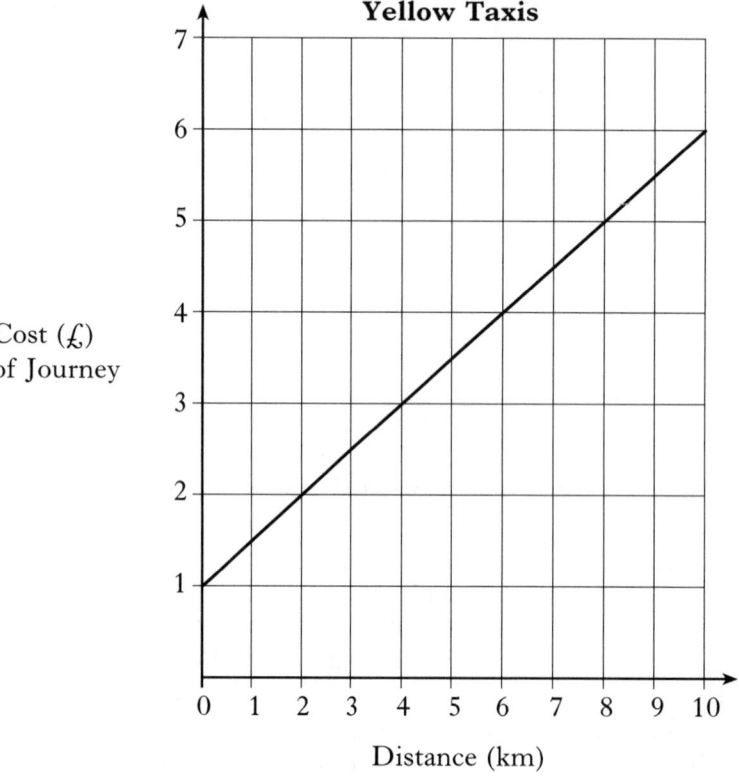

(*a*) How much is the basic charge? **1**

(*b*) How much do Yellow Taxis charge per kilometre? **2**

(*c*) Find the cost of a 12 kilometre taxi journey. **2** **1**

4. (a) On the coordinate diagram below, plot the points

(−7, 0), (−2, −8) and (6, −3).

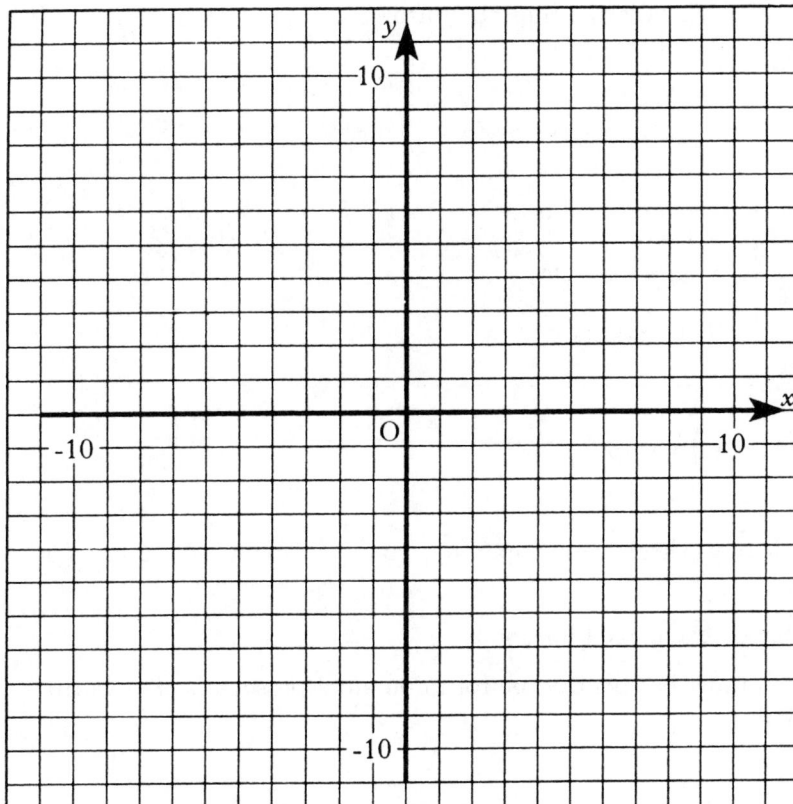

(b) The three points above are three corners of a square.

On the same diagram, plot the point which is the fourth corner of the square.

5. Superbuy Stores have a Friendly card which allows a shopper to collect points for money spent.

One point is given for each whole £1 spent.

(a) Anjum spends £27·26 in a Superbuy Store.

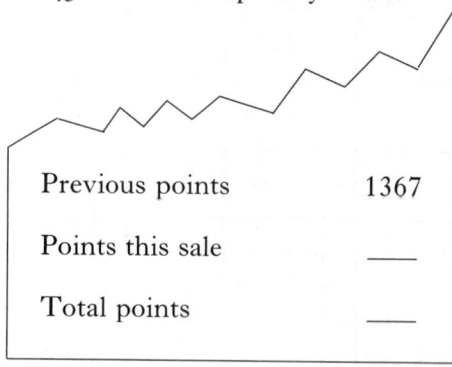

Previous points	1367
Points this sale	____
Total points	____

Complete his till receipt.

(b) When you buy petrol from Superbuy, you get 3 points for every £5 spent.

Points may be exchanged for goods.

How much must be spent on petrol to obtain a personal stereo worth 380 points?

6. (a) Solve the inequality

$$2(x + 3) < 18.$$

(b) Factorise

$$15 - 10x.$$

7. A sculpture is to be made by stacking three blocks of stone.
Each block of stone is a cube of side $(1 \cdot 2 \pm 0 \cdot 05)$ metres.

What is the maximum height of the sculpture?

8. A group of hillwalkers decided to climb a hill.
The graph shows their speed from the start of their climb until they reached the top of the hill.

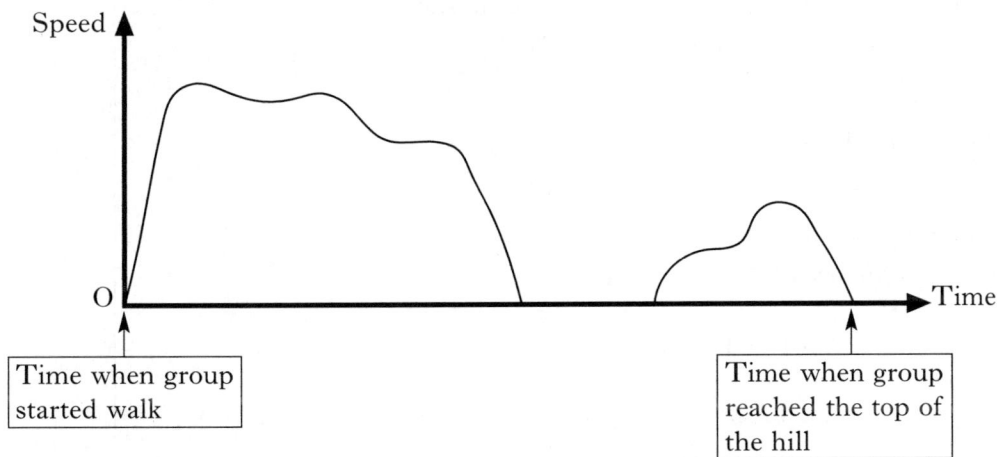

Two hours after starting the climb, the group stopped for lunch.

Use the graph to estimate how long the group stopped for lunch.

Model Paper C

PAPER 2

Calculators may be used in this paper.

1. Salvatore is going back to Italy to visit his parents.
   He wants to exchange £160 into Lire.

Country	Rate per £
Austria	16·70 Schillings
France	8·15 Francs
Greece	365·00 Drachmas
Italy	2390·00 Lire
Spain	196·58 Pesetas

   How many Lire will he get?

2. A mobile phone company lists its charges as follows.

Phone Rental	£12·75 per month
Peak rate calls	42p per minute
Off-peak calls	18p per minute
+ VAT at 17·5%	

   Complete this phone bill.

Rental for 1 month	£12·75
296 minutes at peak rate	£
183 minutes at off-peak rate	£
VAT at 17·5 %	£
TOTAL	

3. Class 3F took part in a sponsored swim for school funds.

The frequency table below shows the number of lengths completed by each pupil in Class 3F.

No. of lengths	No. of pupils
5	3
6	8
7	5
8	6
9	4
10	4

(a) Calculate:
   (i) the mean number of lengths by the class;
   (ii) the mode for this distribution.

(b) Write down the probability that a pupil from 3F completed 10 lengths.

4. A garden centre sells wire frames to support tall flowering plants.

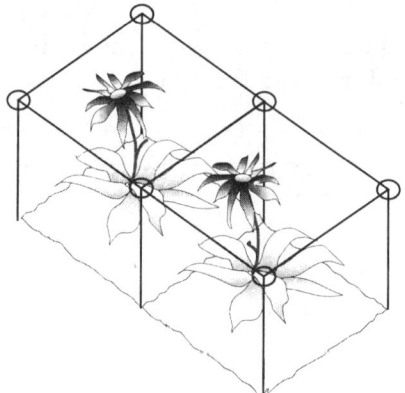

The frames consist of identical squares which are held up by metal rods through the holes at the corners.

Rows of flowers can be supported by placing squares in a straight line. Two different frames are shown in the diagram below.

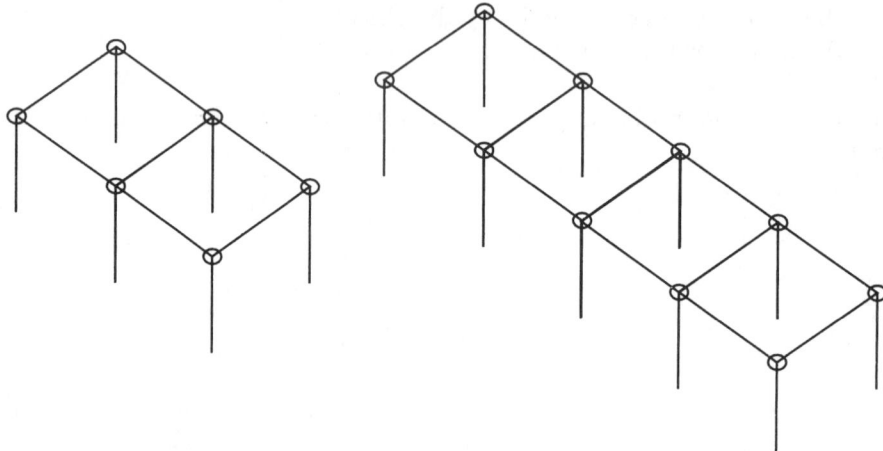

The frame with two squares needs 6 rods, one for each hole.

(a) Complete the table below to show the numbers of rods needed for different numbers of squares.

Number of Squares (N)	1	2	3	4	5	6
Number of Rods (R)		6				

(b) Write down a formula for the number of rods, R, needed for N squares.

$$R = $$

(c) Each square has a side of 30 centimetres.
How many squares and how many rods are needed to support a row of flowers 6 metres long?

5. This advertisement appeared in a newspaper.

STRATHCLYDE THEATRE

	ADULT	CHILD
Balcony	£12	£8
Front Stalls	£10	£6
Back Stalls	£8	£5

Phone for details of
Special Prices for Mid-week Show

A school telephoned for details of the special prices for the mid-week show.

Tickets for seats in the back stalls were bought for 20 pupils and 2 teachers.

The tickets cost a total of £60.

(a) How much did the school save?

(b) The teachers paid £5 each for their tickets.

How much did each pupil's ticket cost?

6. The opening of the fireplace, shown in the diagram below, consists of a rectangle and a semi-circle.

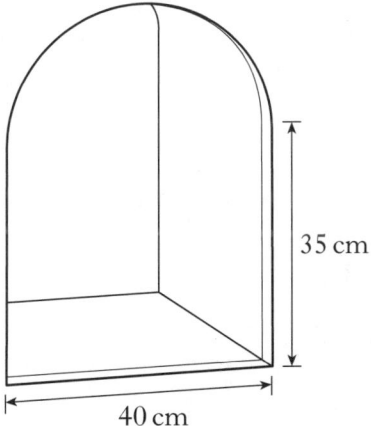

A metal strip is to be placed around the fireplace opening.

Calculate the length of the metal strip.

7. The weight of 20 newborn chickens (to the nearest gram) are given below.

| 42 | 37 | 55 | 31 | 40 | 45 | 63 | 38 | 50 | 47 |
| 55 | 39 | 44 | 53 | 79 | 40 | 54 | 61 | 49 | 47 |

Draw a stem-and-leaf diagram to illustrate this data.

8. Crossflags golf club has a new logo.

It is formed by rotating the shape in the diagram through 90° about the point marked O.

Complete the logo.

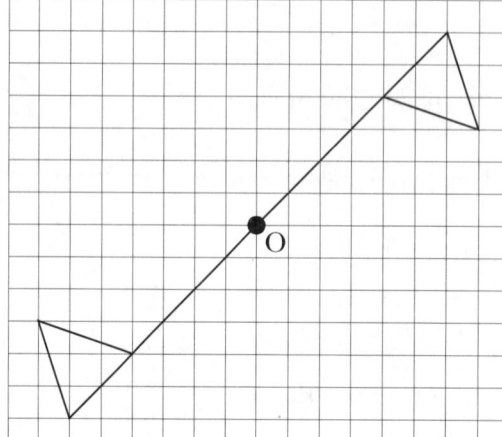

9. The diagram below shows the positions of three towns, Belford, Hoylake and Liston.

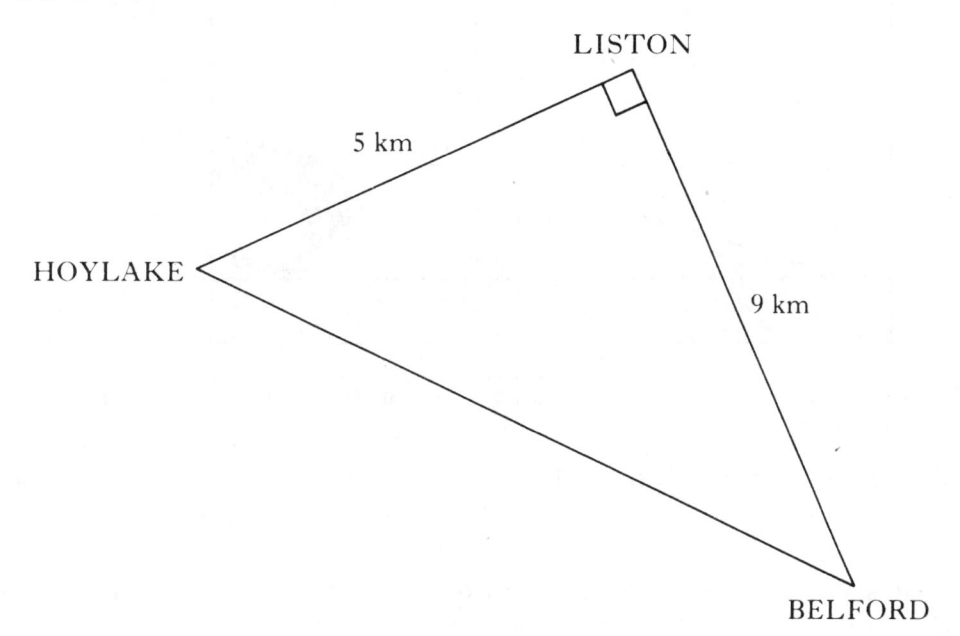

LISTON

5 km

HOYLAKE

9 km

BELFORD

Calculate the distance from Hoylake to Belford.

Give your answer correct to 1 decimal place.

10. The drawing shows part of a map.

The two dots represent hilltops.

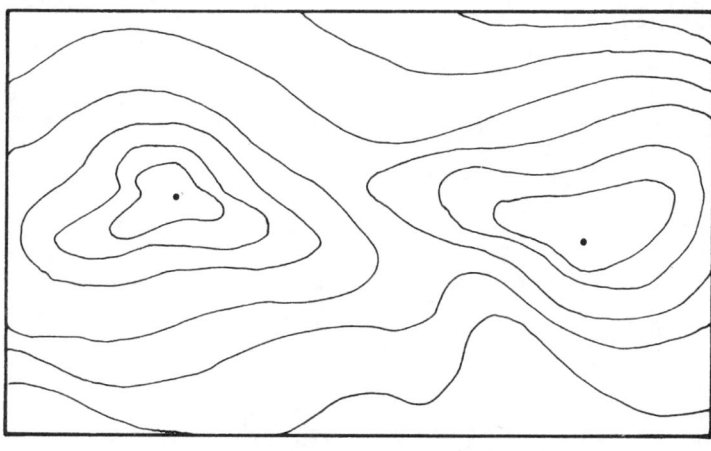

SCALE 1:50 000

(a) Measure the distance between the dots on the map.

(b) Use the scale to calculate the actual distance between the hilltops.

Give your answer in kilometres.

11. The sketch below shows a ramp at the back of a removal van.

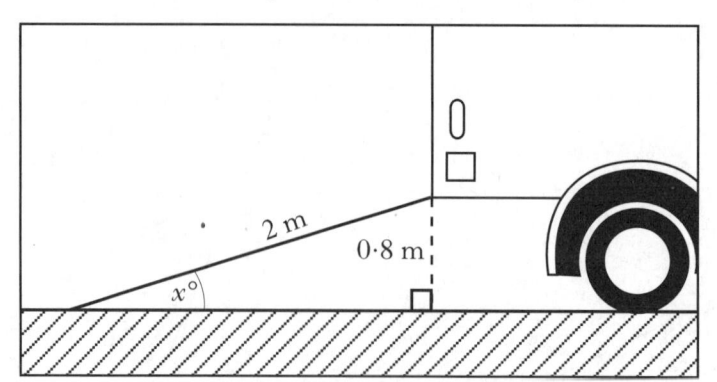

The ramp is 2 metres long and is fixed to the van 0·8 metres above the ground.

Calculate the size of the angle marked $x°$.

12. Mike and Alan are doing an experiment to show that the weight of a steel bar, W grams, varies directly with its length, L centimetres.

The table below shows their results.

Length of bar (L centimetres)	3·2	4·8	10	16	18·4	22
Weight of Bar (W grams)	40	60	125	200	230	275

Explain how these results can be used to find out if the weight of the bar varies directly with its length.

13.

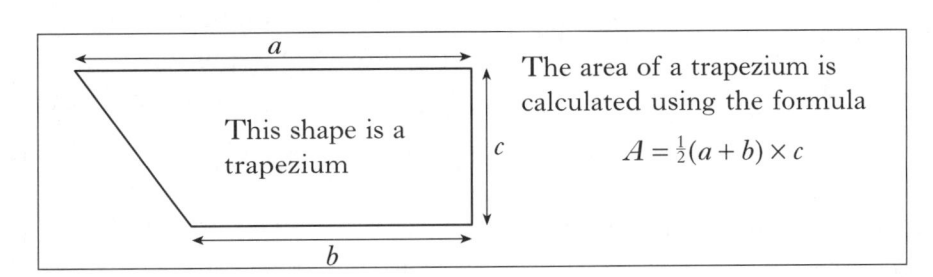

This shape is a trapezium

The area of a trapezium is calculated using the formula

$$A = \tfrac{1}{2}(a+b) \times c$$

The diagram below shows part of a rainwater gutter.

The ends of the gutter are identical.

Each end is in the shape of a trapezium.

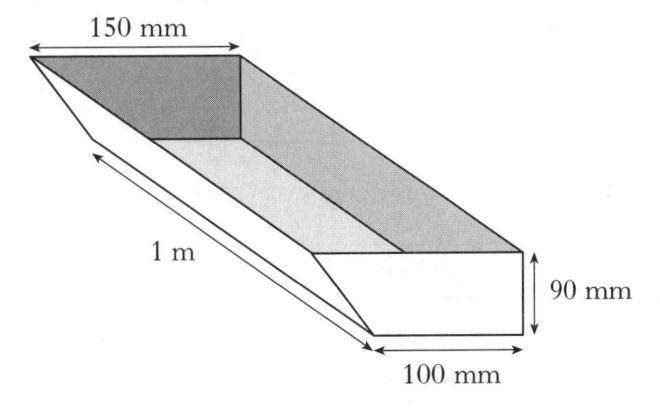

150 mm

1 m

90 mm

100 mm

Calculate the **volume** of this part of the gutter.

[END OF QUESTION PAPER]

NATIONAL
QUALIFICATIONS
MODEL PAPER D

MATHEMATICS
STANDARD GRADE
General Level
Paper 1
(Non-calculator)

1. Carry out the following calculations
   (a) 54×39
   (b) $5 \times (-7)$
   (c) $2 \cdot 04 \times 400$
   (d) $1 \cdot 845 \div 3$.

2. The depth of a submarine was noted every three hours.

Time	noon	3 pm	6 pm	9 pm	midnight
Depth in metres	−60	−17	−28	0	−23

Complete the table below to show the change in depth of the submarine.

Time interval	Change in depth
Noon to 3 pm	up 43 metres
3 pm to 6 pm	
6 pm to 9 pm	
9 pm to midnight	

3. The table below shows the distance in miles between different places in Scotland.

EDINBURGH					
48	GLASGOW				
158	165	INVERNESS			
45	62	113	PERTH		
56	8	173	70	PAISLEY	
124	85	250	145	75	STRANRAER

(a) Use the table above to find the distance from Edinburgh to Paisley.

(b) Allan is a salesman whose office is in Edinburgh.

He gets travelling expenses at the rate of 27·5 pence per mile.

On Monday he travels from Edinburgh to Paisley and back.

How much does he get in travelling expenses?

(c) Each year, **after** he has travelled 8000 miles, Allan's expenses are reduced to 16·2 pence per mile.

In 1997, Allan travelled 9200 miles altogether.

What were his **total** travelling expenses for 1997?

4. The two shapes below are reflected in the line AB.

Draw the new positions of the two shapes.

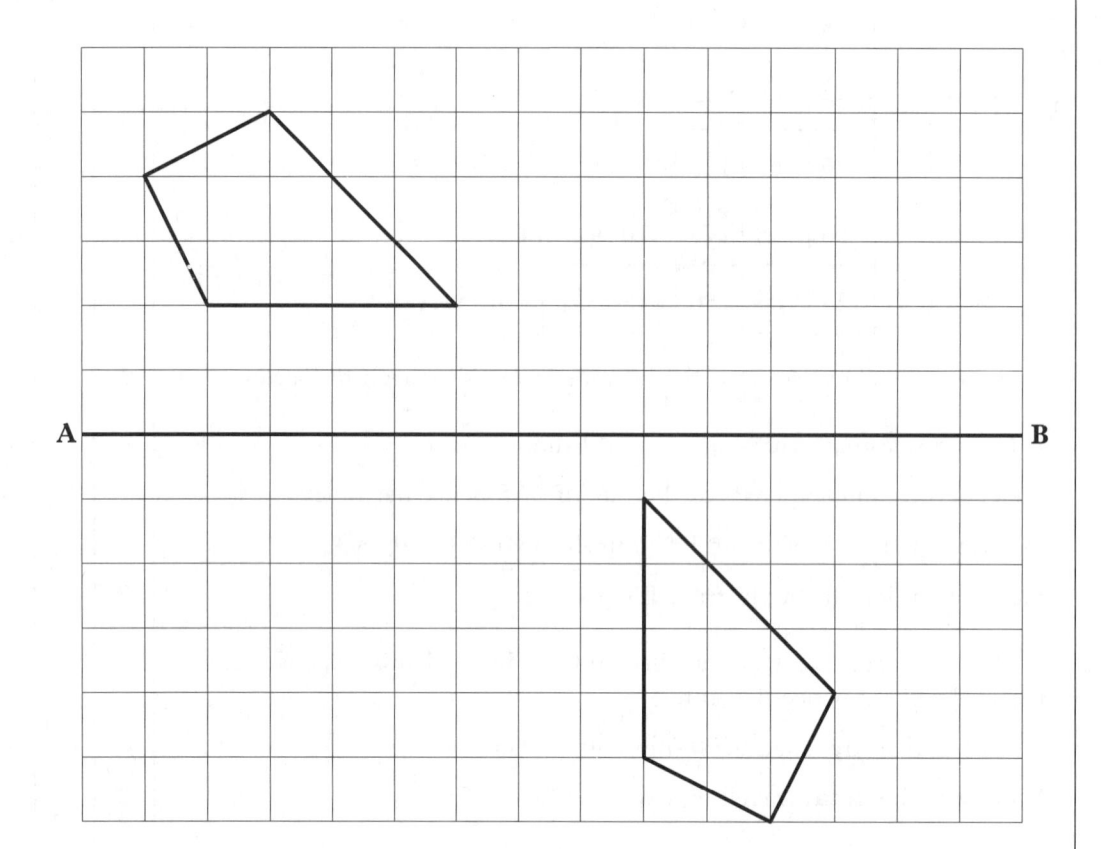

5. Three friends set off on an 820 kilometre journey.

They travel at an average speed of 80 kilometres per hour.

How long will the journey take?

Give your answer in hours and minutes.

6. (a) Solve **algebraically** the inequality

$$7y + 3 < -4.$$

(b) Factorise $15w + 6st$.

7. The diagram below shows a kite PQRS and a circle with centre Q.
PS is the tangent to the circle at P and RS is the tangent to the circle at R.

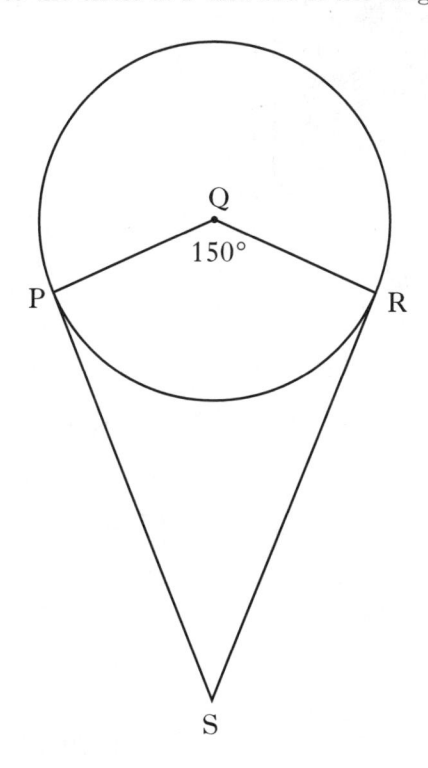

(a) What is the size of angle QRS?

(b) Calculate the size of angle PSR

8. To get money from a cash machine you need an appropriate card and a four digit Personal Identity Number (PIN).

David knows:
- his PIN contains the digits 2, 5, 6 and 9;
- 2 is the first digit.

One possible PIN is shown in the table below.

Complete the table to show all the possible PINs.

2	5	6	9

9. There are 52 cards in a standard pack of playing cards.

If there are 13 cards in each of the 4 'suits', spades, clubs, hearts and diamonds, and there is a five in each of the suits, what is the probability of choosing a 5 at random from a pack of cards?

Model Paper D

PAPER 2

Calculators may be used in this paper.

1.
EXCHANGE RATES for £1 Sterling		
FRANCE	8·92	francs
GERMANY	2·65	marks
GREECE	426	drachmas
ITALY	2650	lire
SPAIN	220	pesetas

   (a) Scott goes on holiday to Spain.

   He buys a camera costing 9900 pesetas.

   How much is this in pounds sterling?

   (b) The same camera costs 121·9 marks in Germany and 18 531 drachmas in Greece.

   In which of the three countries is the camera cheapest?

2. One video costs £13·50.
   On Special Offer is a set of 8 videos costing £104.

   1 VIDEO — £13·50

   SPECIAL OFFER

   8-VIDEO SET—£104

   (a) How much is saved by buying the set?

   (b) Express the saving as a percentage of the cost of 8 single videos.

3. The temperature (°C) at the summit on two Scottish mountains was recorded over a 7-day period during the busy skiing season.

Mountain 1	−4	1	−2	0	2	−1	−3
Mountain 2	−2	0	−3	1	2	−1	

The final reading for Mountain 2 is missing.

(a) Calculate the average temperature at the summit of Mountain 1 over this 7-day period.

(b) If both summits had the same average temperature over the 7-day period, what is the missing temperature for Mountain 2?

Model Paper D

4. Two lenders, Mortgages Direct and Leading Mortgage, offer mortgages at different rates on a loan of £45 000.

Mortgages Direct

Monthly payment £330.50

Plus

One-off set-up fee £500

Leading Mortgage

Monthly payment £349.90

And

No other fees to pay

Which mortgage would be better value over a period of 3 years and by how much?

5. Amy needs to replace fencing in her garden.

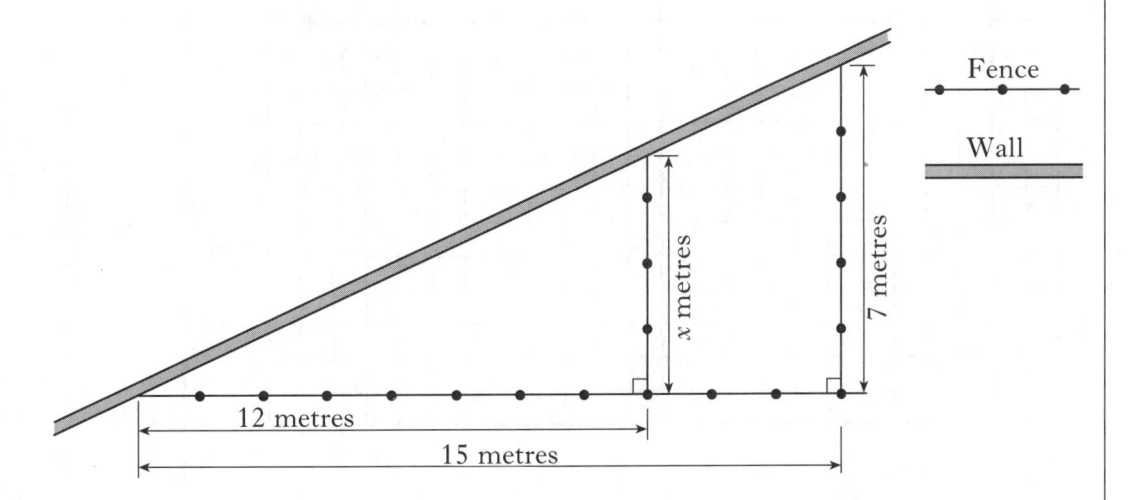

She has taken the measurements shown above, but has forgotten to measure the part of the fence marked x metres.

The garden centre has only 28 metres of fencing in stock.

Is this enough to completely replace the existing fencing?

6. (a) Complete the table below for $y = 2x + 1$.

x	-4	0	4
y			

(b) Using the table in part (a), draw the graph of the line $y = 2x + 1$ on the grid.

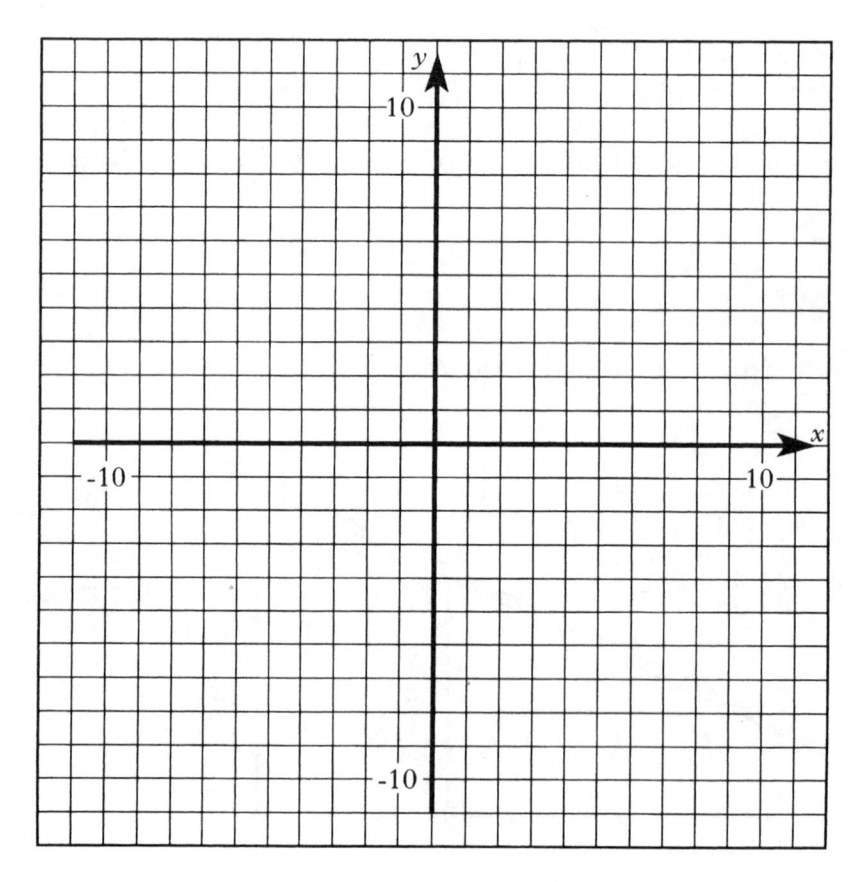

7. A college course is made up of 8 units of work.

Students are graded A, B, C or D on each unit.

Each grade is worth a number of points as shown in the table below.

Grade	Points
A	3
B	2
C	1
D	0

In order to pass the course, students need to

(i) complete all 8 units

and

(ii) score a total of 21 points or more.

One way is shown in the table below.

Number of As	Number of Bs	Number of Cs	Number of Ds	Number of Points
7	–	–	1	21
7	–	1	–	22
7	1	–	–	23
8	–	–	–	24
6	1	1	–	21
6	2	–	–	22
5	3	–	–	21

Fill in the rest of the table to show all the different ways of passing the course.

8. The box for a chocolate bar is shown below.

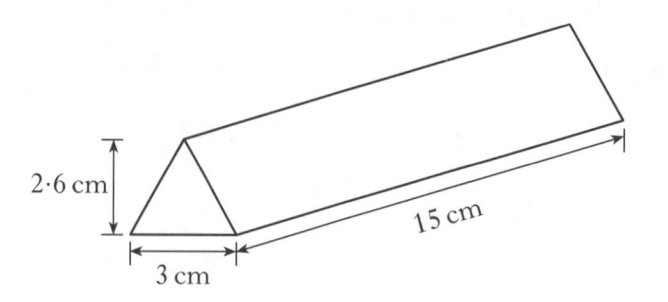

   2·6 cm
   3 cm
   15 cm

   Six chocolate bars are packaged together.

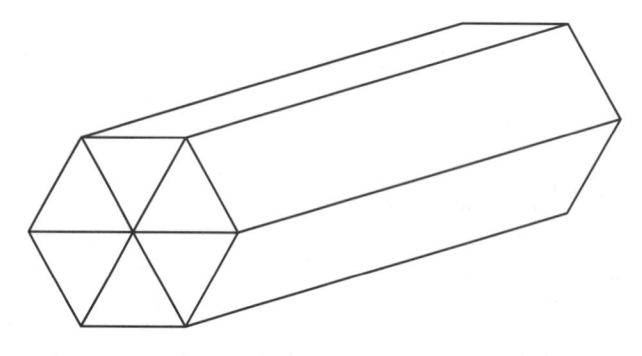

   Find the volume of the package of six bars.

9. The braking distance, D metres, of a motorbike varies directly as the square of its speed, V kilometres per hour.

   The braking distance is 16 m when the speed is 40 km/h.

   Calculate the braking distance when the speed is 60 km/h.

10. The diagram shows a ramp connecting two levels in a shopping centre.

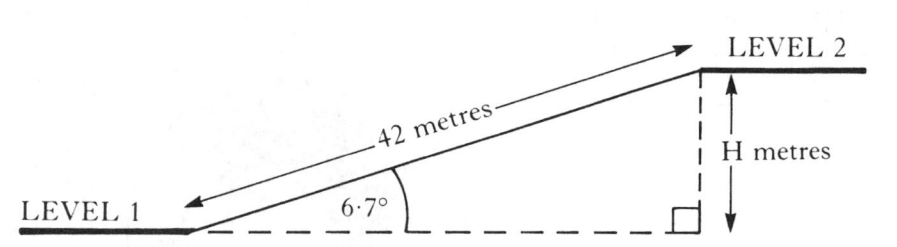

The ramp is 42 metres long, and slopes at an angle of 6·7°, as shown in the diagram.

Calculate the difference in height, H metres, between the two levels.

11. A large box is filled with packets of rice.

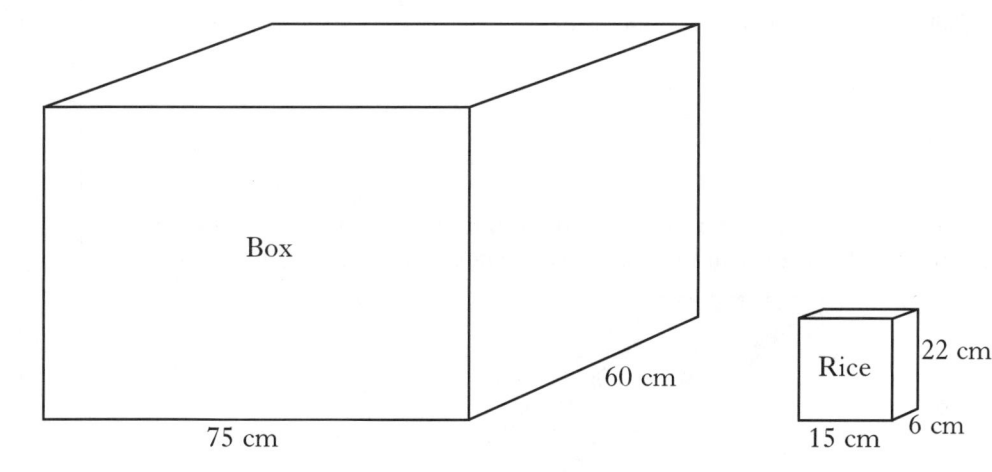

Each packet measures 15 centimetres by 6 centimetres by 22 centimetres and the packets are stacked upright in the box.

(a) How many packets fit exactly into the base of the box?

(b) When full, the box contains 150 packets.

What is the height of the box?

(c) How many boxes could be stacked on top of each other in a space which is 5 metres high?

Show all your working.

12. A satellite travels in a circular orbit round the earth once every $2\frac{1}{2}$ hours.

The satellite is 2900 kilometres above the earth's surface.

The earth has a radius of 6400 kilometres.

(a) What is the radius of the orbit of the satellite?

(b) Calculate the speed of the satellite.

13. A rectangular picture measuring 610 millimetres by 180 millimetres is placed diagonally in a cuboid shaped box as shown in Diagram 1.

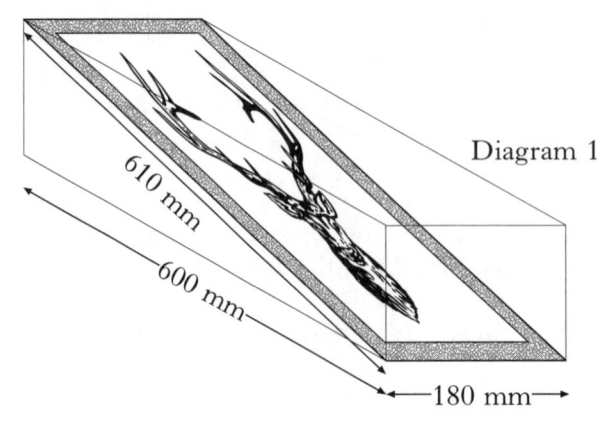

Diagram 1

The box has length 600 millimetres and breadth 180 millimetres.

Calculate the height of the box.

[END OF QUESTION PAPER]

NATIONAL
QUALIFICATIONS
MODEL PAPER E

MATHEMATICS
STANDARD GRADE
General Level
Paper 1
(Non-calculator)

	KU	RE

1. Carry out the following calculations
   (a) 53×22 — KU 2
   (b) $5 - 14\cdot2 + 21\cdot16$ — KU 1
   (c) -9×8 — KU 1
   (d) $2\cdot295 \div 9$. — KU 1

2. $\frac{2}{5}$ of all pupils attending Heritage Academy walk to school.

   There are 475 pupils in the school.

   How many pupils walk to Heritage Academy? — KU 2

3. The distance from the earth to the sun is $1\cdot58 \times 10^{-5}$ light years.

   Write this number in full. — KU 2

4. The graph shows the monthly attendances at a water leisure centre from January 1990 to January 1993.

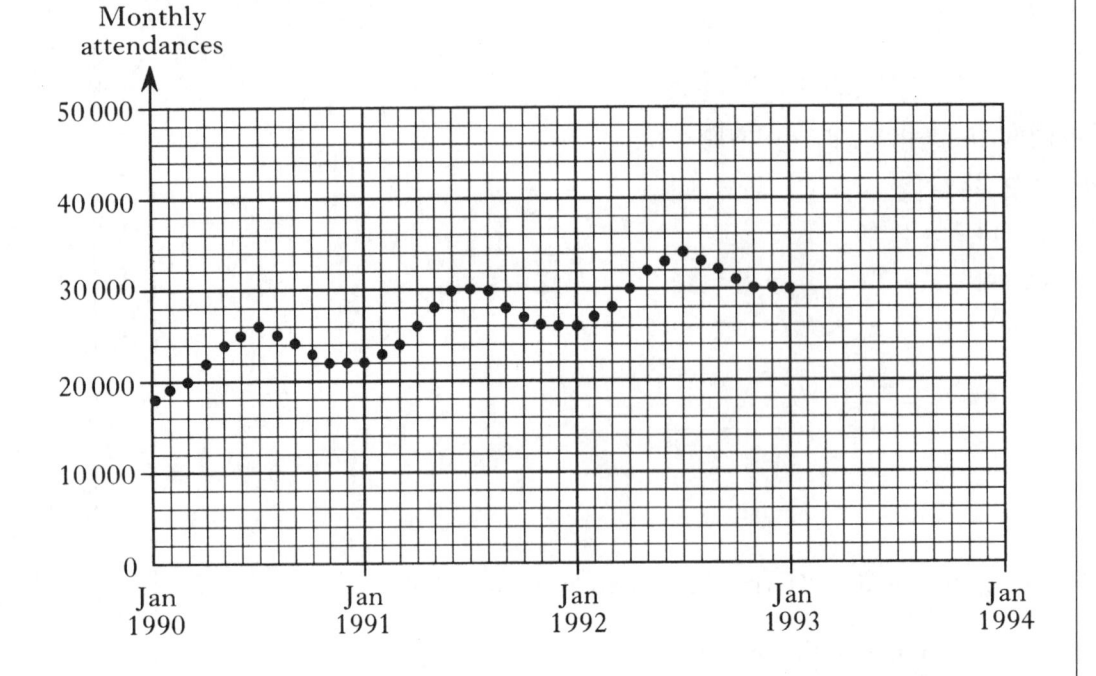

(a) Describe the **overall** trend of the graph.

(b) Describe what happened to the attendances from January 1992 to January 1993.

(c) Estimate the attendance in July 1993.

5. This table shows insurance premiums for holidays abroad.

INSURANCE PREMIUM per person				
	Europe		*Rest of the World*	
Duration of Holiday	Adult* (16–64)	Child (0–15)	Adult* (16–64)	Child (0–15)
Up to 8 days	£27·50	£19·50	£42·50	£37·50
9–16 days	£35·00	£30·00	£51·20	£47·00
17–24 days	£39·50	£35·00	£60·20	£56·00
* Premiums double for persons 65 years and over				

Mr and Mrs Jones, both 35 years old, take their two children, aged 3 and 8, and Mr Jones's father, aged 70, on a one week holiday to Europe.

Find the total cost of the insurance premium.

6. (*a*) Tamara, Eva and Katrina are sisters.

Eva and Katrina are twins.

Tamara is 3 years older than the twins.

The total of the sisters' ages is 42 years.

Form an equation using the above information.

(*b*) Solve the equation to find Tamara's age.

7. The diagram shows a Magic Triangle.

It is "magic" because the total of the numbers along each of the three sides is the same.

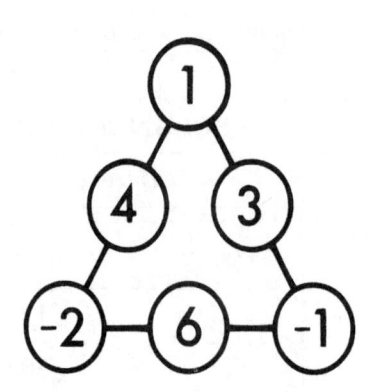

(a) What is the total for one side of this triangle?

(b) Use the numbers −2, −1, 1 and 2 to complete the magic triangle below, where the total for each side is 2.

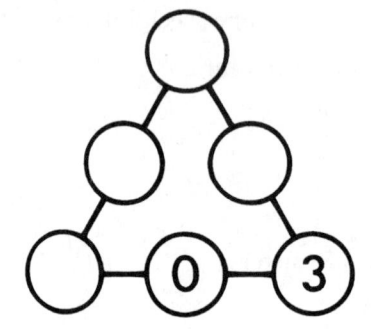

8. A company makes rectangular cards of different sizes. The cards are coded according to their size.

R1 is 1 centimetre by 2 centimetres.

R2 is 2 centimetres by 3 centimetres.

R3 is 3 centimetres by 4 centimetres

and so on.

(a) Write down the size of the next card, R4.

(b) How many R4 pieces of card can be cut from an R10 piece of card? You must explain your answer.

PAPER 2

Calculators may be used in this paper.

1. John is a diabetic who has to monitor his blood sugar level on a daily basis. His blood sugar levels over a 14 day period were

    4·9   6·1   5·6   8·4   6·3   7·4   4·3
    6·7   7·8   7·9   5·8   9·3   8·1   7·0

    Calculate his average blood sugar level over the 14 days, giving your answer correct to 1 decimal place.

2. Two garages are selling the same model of car for the same price.

    One garage asks for a £500 deposit and 12 equal payments of £750.

    The other garage asks for a £1100 deposit and 24 equal payments.

    How much should each payment be?

3. Alan and David are brothers.
Their journeys from home to school are shown on the graph below.

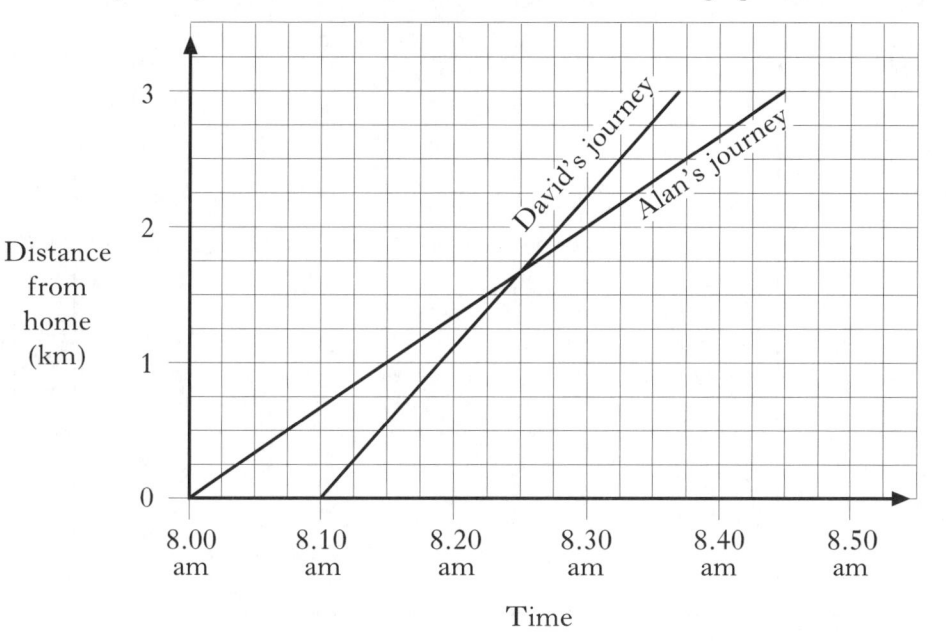

Distance from home (km) vs *Time*, with David's journey and Alan's journey plotted.

(a) At what time do the brothers meet on their way to school?

(b) How far is the school from their home?

(c) Calculate Alan's average speed for the journey.

Give your answer in kilometres per hour.

4. A new cinema with 760 seats has just opened.

During the first week, the cinema was open 7 days and ran 3 showings per day.

A total of 11 530 tickets was sold.

The cinema manager has been set a target of selling at least 70% of the tickets for the first week.

Did the manager meet the target?

You must explain your answer.

5. Part of a straight line graph is shown below.

The line can be extended in either direction.

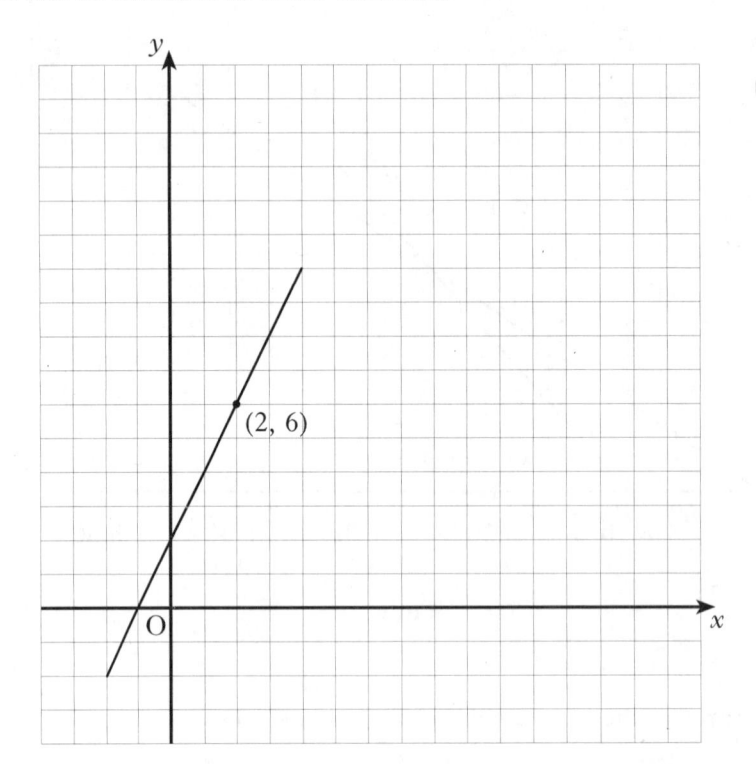

(a) Complete the table below to show the coordinates of some of the points on the straight line.

x	1	2	3	4	5	6
y		6				

(b) Write down a formula for finding y when you know x.

$$y =$$

(c) The point $(a, 22)$ lies on the straight line.

Find a.

6.

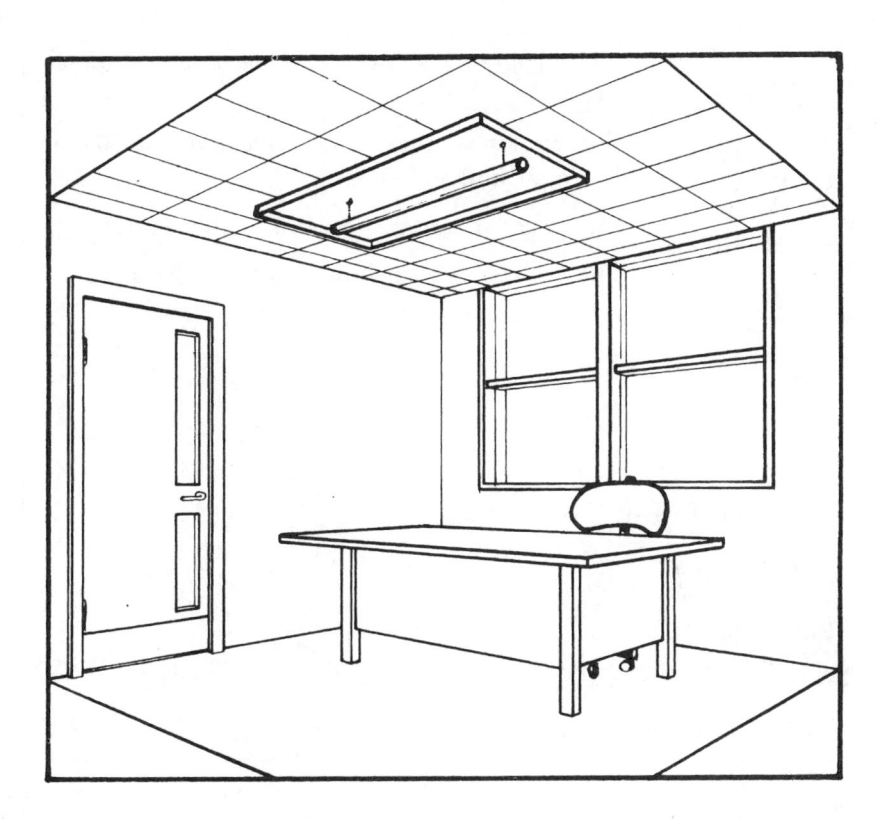

The amount of light needed in an office depends on its room index, R.

$$R = \frac{LW}{H(L + W)}$$

where   L metres is the length of the office,
W metres is the width of the office,
H metres is the height of the light above the desk.

Calculate the room index for an office 5·5 metres long and 4·2 metres wide, with the light 1·3 metres above the desk.

7. The diagram shows a Coastguard's radar screen.

The circles on the screen have radii of 10 km, 20 km, 30 km, and 40 km.

On the radar screen, port P is at the centre.

The yacht Y is also shown on the radar screen.

(a) Plot the position of yacht Y on the map.

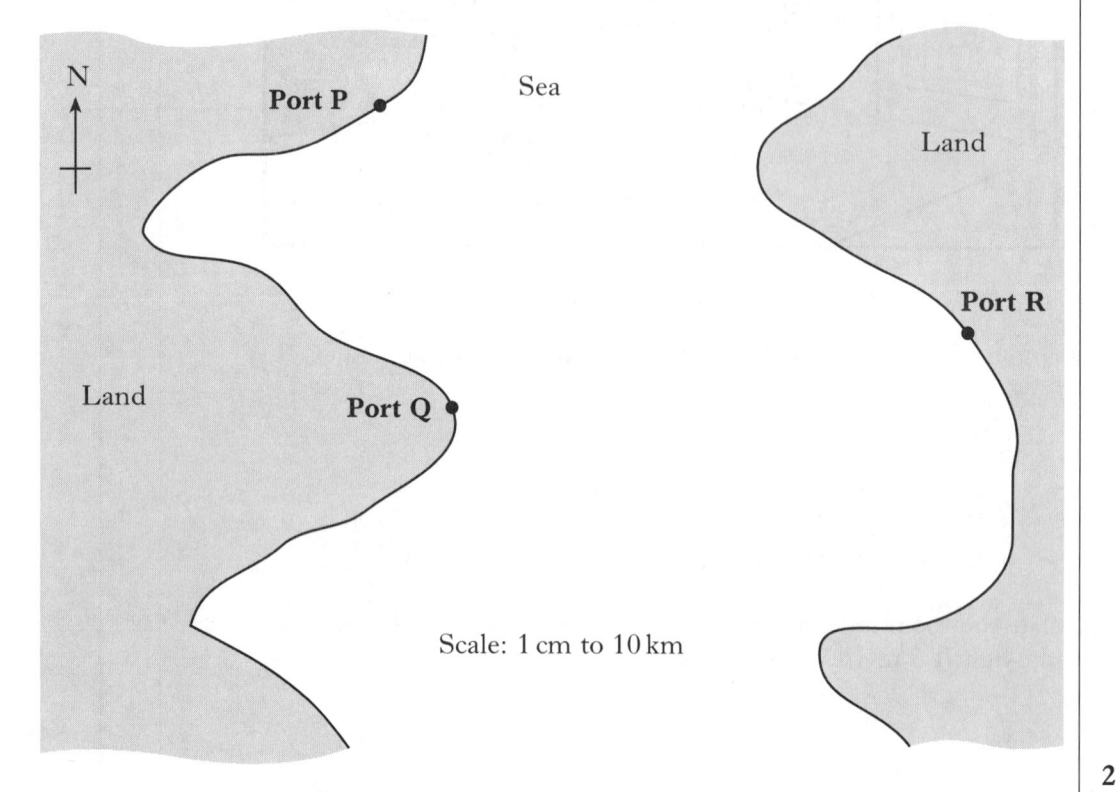

Scale: 1 cm to 10 km

(b) The Coastguard receives a warning of bad weather and advises the yacht to sail to the nearest port.

To which port should the yacht sail?

Give a reason for your answer.

(c) Find the bearing and the distance from the yacht to the nearest port.

Model Paper E

8. There are 49 different numbers from 1 to 49 which can be drawn at random in the National Lottery.

(a) How many of these numbers are even?

(b) What is the probability that the first number drawn will be 49?

(c) What is the probability that the first number drawn will be odd?

9. A wall display cabinet is made in the shape of an equilateral triangle with length of side 40 centimetres.

One half of the cabinet has shelves; the other half has a glass door.

(a) Calculate the height of the cabinet.

(b) Find the area of the glass door.

10. The distance to the horizon, d kilometres, varies as the square root of the height, h metres, above sea level.

The distance to the horizon is 14·4 kilometres at a height of 16 metres above sea level.

Calculate the distance to the horizon at a height of 25 metres above sea level.

11. The design of a trolley wheel is shown. The manufacturer requires that **angle x must be more than 32°**.

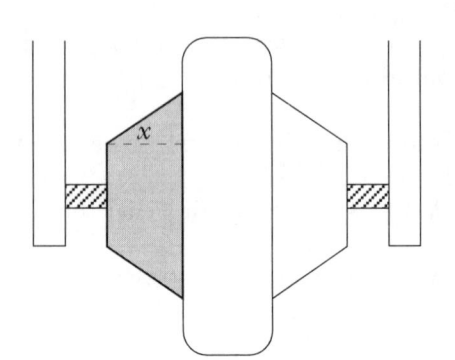

Part of this design has measurements as shown.

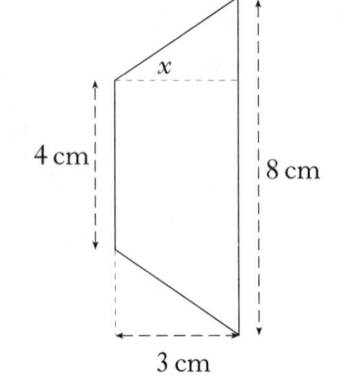

Do these measurements satisfy the manufacturer's requirements?

Give a reason for your answer.

Do not use a scale drawing.

4

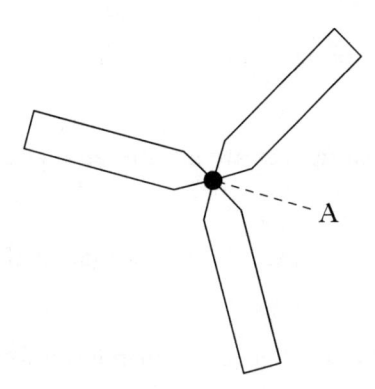

12.

The logo above has rotational symmetry of **order 3** about point A.

Part of a company logo is shown below.

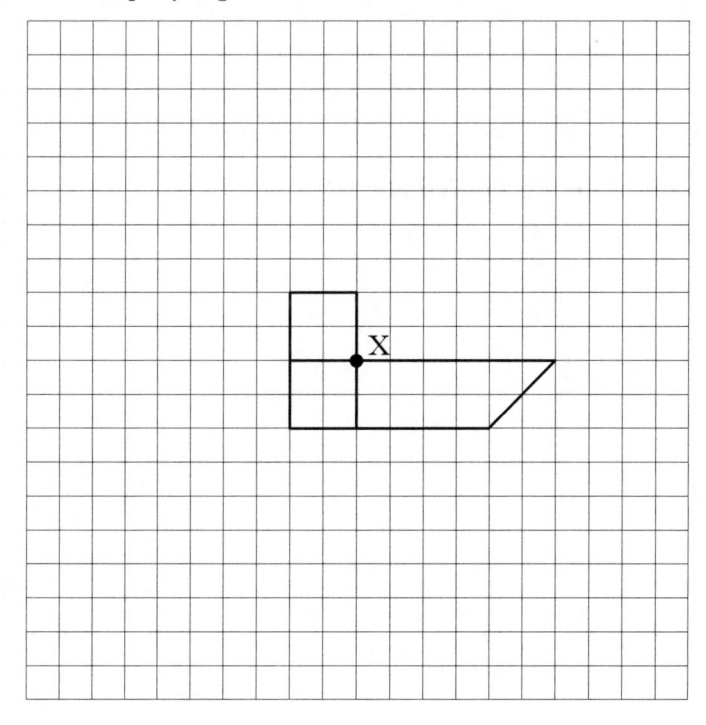

Complete the logo so that it has rotational symmetry of order 4 about point X.

3

13. Anne is trying to guess Martin's phone number. She knows it has four figures.

Martin tells Anne that the first three figures are all the same and that the sum of all four figures is 15.

(a) Write down all the possible four-figure numbers that fit the description of Martin's phone number.

(b) Martin now tells Anne that the last figure is a prime number.

Write down Martin's phone number.

[*END OF QUESTION PAPER*]

NATIONAL
QUALIFICATIONS
MODEL PAPER F

MATHEMATICS
STANDARD GRADE
General Level
Paper 1
(Non-calculator)

	KU	RE

1. Carry out the following calculations
   (a) 40% of 85 g — 2
   (b) $9 - 11·02 + 13·5$ — 1
   (c) $1·07 \times 200$ — 1
   (d) $64·72 \div 8$. — 1

2. A record store noted that $\frac{5}{6}$ of all CDs sold were from the Top Ten. 696 CDs were sold during the first week of June.

   How many of these would you expect to be from the Top Ten? — 2

3. The operation ✦ means "square the first number and multiply by the second".

   For example, $5 ✦ 3 = 5^2 \times 3 = 25 \times 3 = 75$

   (a) Evaluate $6 ✦ 4$. — 1
   (b) If $a ✦ 5 = 245$, find a. — 2

Model Paper F

4. (a) On the grid below, plot the points

A(1, 6),　　B(4,–2)　　and　　C(1, –4).

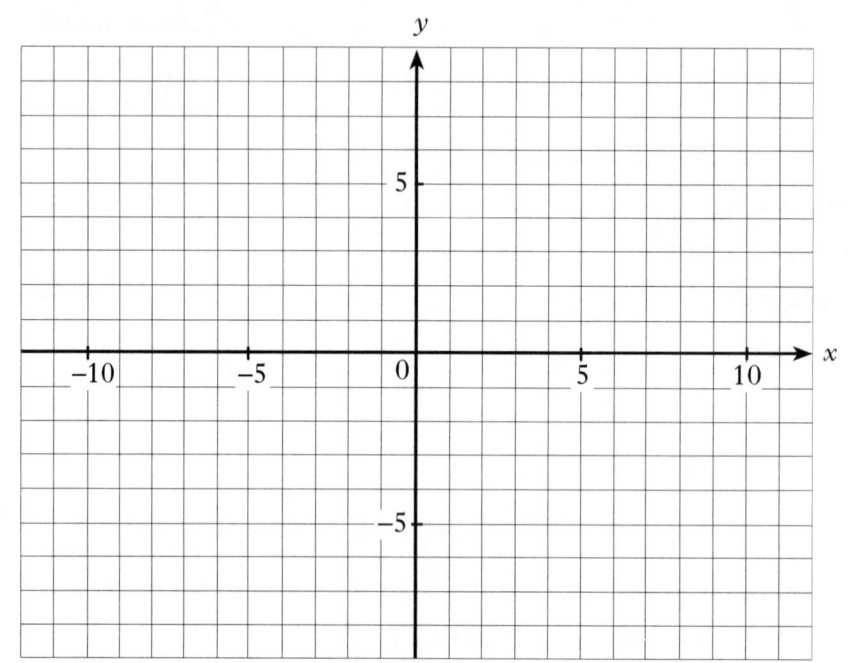

(b) Plot the point D so that ABCD forms a kite.

5. This is part of a tiling of **congruent** kites.

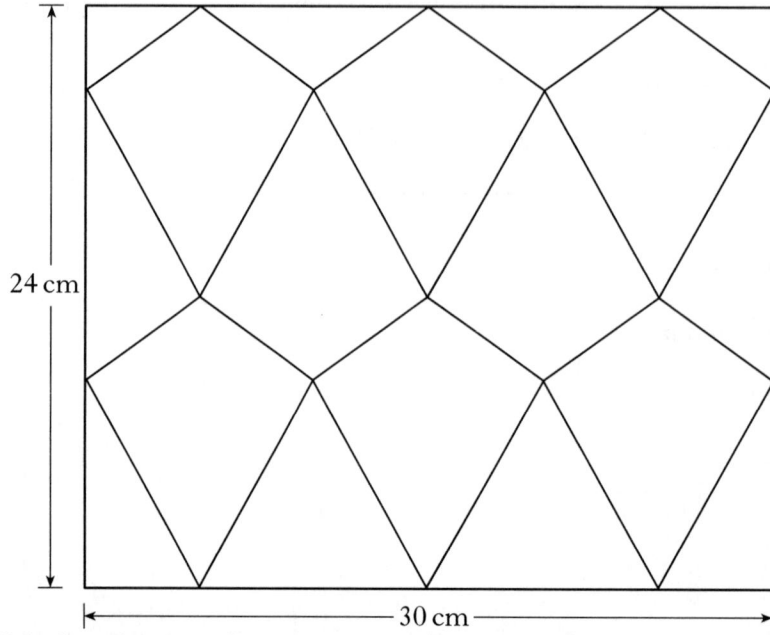

Calculate the area of one kite.

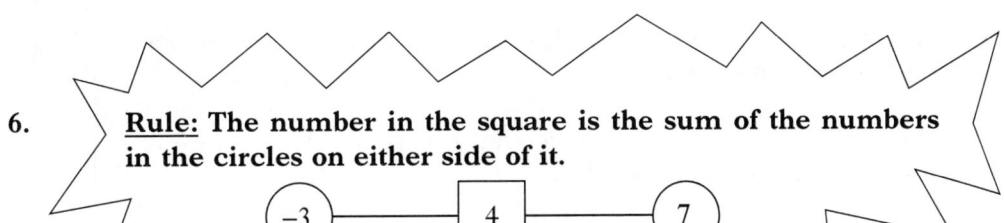

6. **Rule:** The number in the square is the sum of the numbers in the circles on either side of it.

(−3) — [4] — (7)

(a) Use this rule to complete the diagram below.

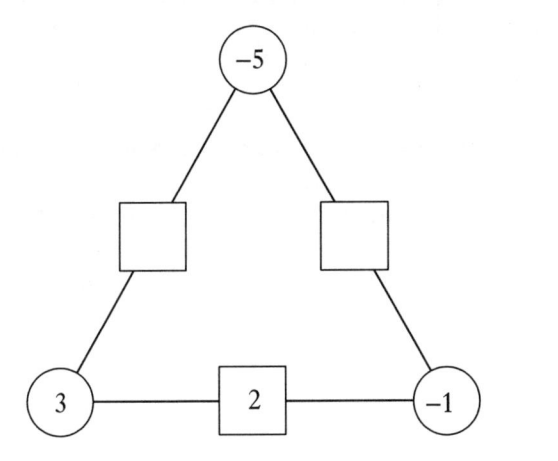

(b) Using the rule, enter the numbers −2, −1, 1, and 3 in the diagram below.

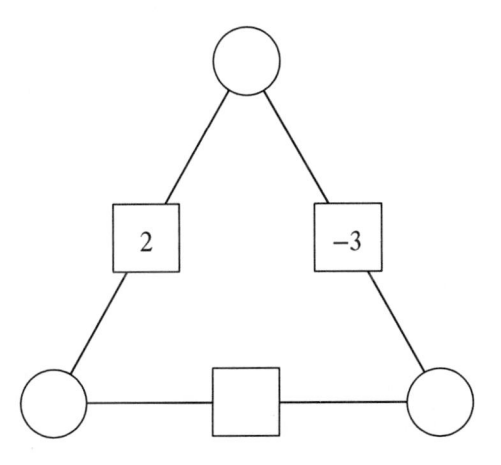

7. Shareen works flexitime in an office. This means that she can choose her starting and finishing times each day.

One week she plans to leave work early on Friday so she works the following hours on Monday to Thursday.

Day of the Week	Start Time	Finish Time	Time Taken for Lunch
Monday	9.00 am	5.30 pm	45 minutes
Tuesday	9.00 am	5.30 pm	45 minutes
Wednesday	9.00 am	5.30 pm	45 minutes
Thursday	9.00 am	5.30 pm	45 minutes

Note: Lunchtimes are not counted as part of working hours.

On Friday she starts work at 9.00 am and does not take a lunch break.

If Shareen wants to work exactly 35 hours this week, when should she leave work on Friday?

4

8. (a) Multiply out the bracket and simplify

$$5(3x + 2y) - 4x.$$

2

(b) Solve algebraically the equation

$$7x + 3 = 2x + 15.$$

2

9.

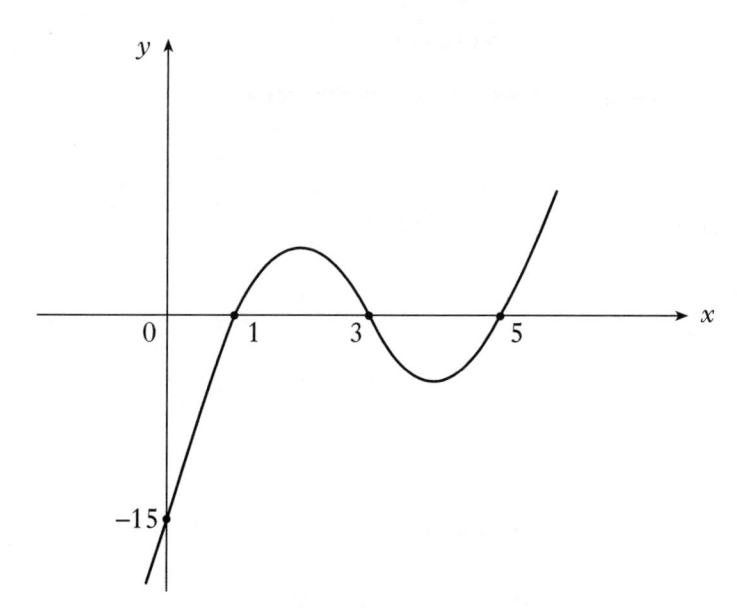

The diagram above shows the graph whose equation is $y = (x-1)(x-3)(x-5)$.

Write down an equation for each of the graphs below.

(a)

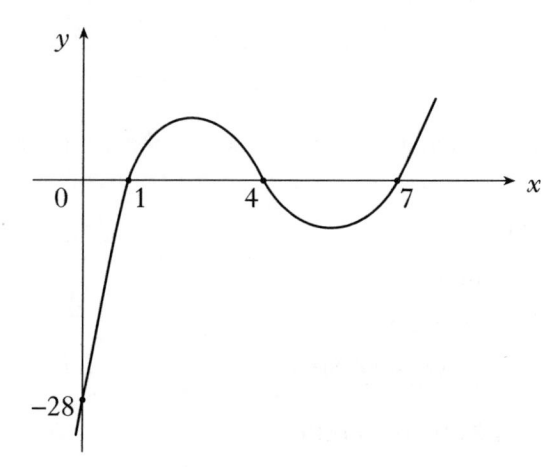

(b)

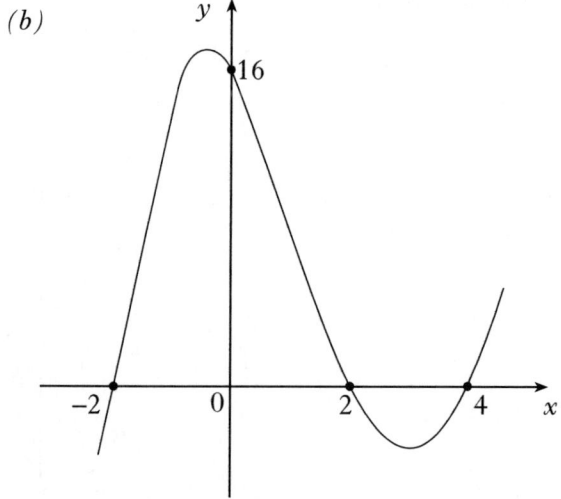

Model Paper F

PAPER 2

Calculators may be used in this paper.

1. The stem-and-leaf diagram below shows the number of people using a Bank's automatic cash machine over a period of 13 days.

    ```
    3 | 1 7
    4 | 0 3 3 4
    5 | 1 8 9         5 / 1 means 51
    6 | 0 2
    7 | 1 3
    ```

    (a) What is the median of this distribution?

    (b) What was the least number of people on any one day?

    (c) Calculate the average number of people using the cash machine over the 13 days, giving your answer correct to 1 decimal place.

2. Mr and Mrs Donaldson are having a party to celebrate their 25th Wedding Anniversary.

    They want to buy Champagne.

    They see this sign in a shop window.

    > **CHAMPAGNE**
    >
    > £24·99 per bottle
    >
    > *15% Discount when you buy 6 bottles*

    Calculate the cost of 6 bottles.

3. John is starting to lay concrete foundations for a garden wall.

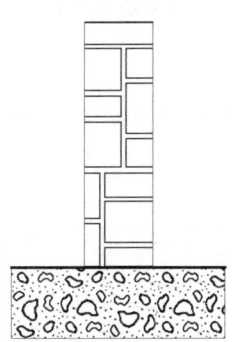

Concrete is made from stones, sand and cement, to which water is added.

He will mix stones and sand in the ratio 3 to 1.

(a) John needs 1·8 cubic metres of stones for the job.

How much sand will he need?

(b) One bag of sand has a volume of 0·075 cubic metres.

How many bags of sand should he buy for the job?

4. Mr and Mrs Tang are visiting Scotland and decide to hire a car for a week.

The car hire company has two different schemes for hiring a car, the Freedom and the Rover.

FREEDOM
£205
per week
All inclusive

ROVER
£145
per week
Plus
6 pence per mile

(a) Complete the table below to show the hire costs for different distances.

Number of miles	0	250	500	750	1000	1250	1500
"FREEDOM": cost in £							
"ROVER": cost in £							

(b) (i) On the grid below, draw a graph to show the hire costs using the Freedom scheme.

(ii) On the same grid, draw a graph showing the Rover hire costs.

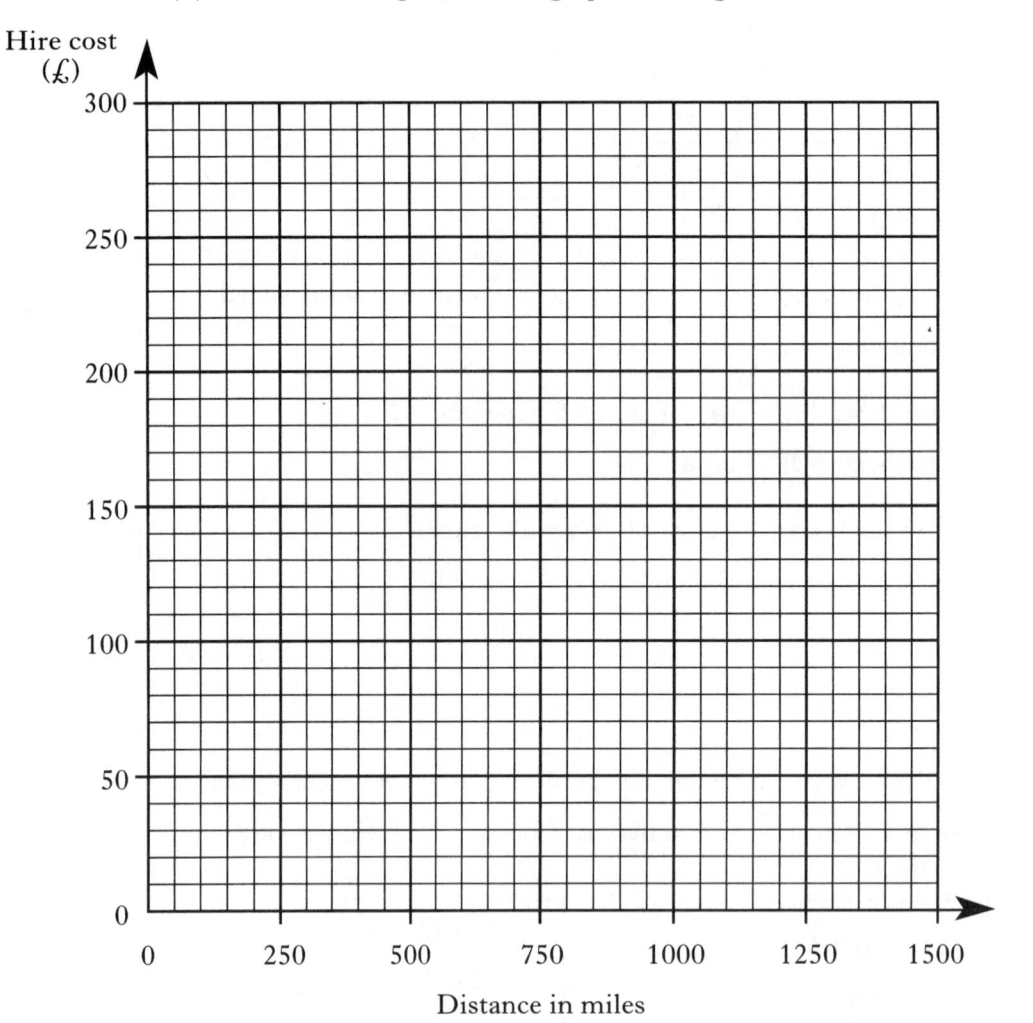

(c) Mr and Mrs Tang plan to drive about 200 miles every day.

Which scheme would be better for them?

Give a reason.

5. The diagram below shows the shape of a traffic sign.

It consists of a rectangle and a triangle.

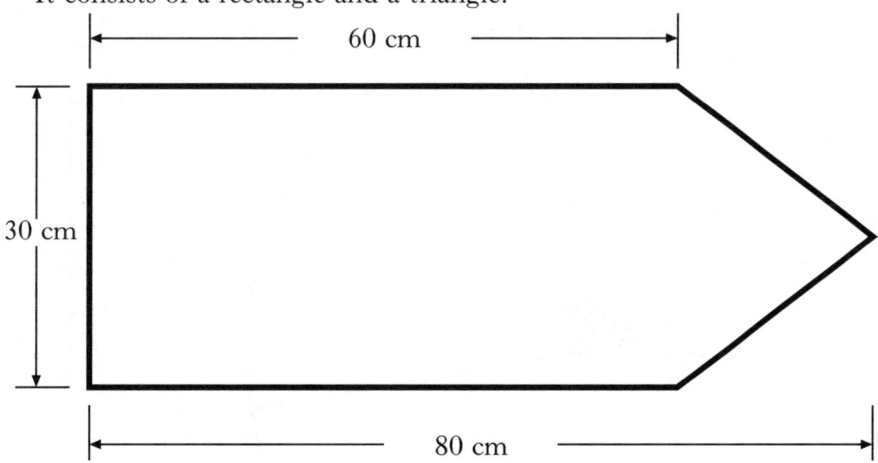

[Diagram: rectangle 60 cm by 30 cm with a triangle on the right; total length 80 cm]

Calculate the area of the shape.

6. The percentage of softening agents in any fabric conditioner must be between 15% and 30% for it to be effective.

A 640 ml sample of Ocean, a new fabric conditioner, was found to contain 128 ml of softening agents.

Is Ocean an effective fabric conditioner?

Give a reason for your answer.

7. The pie chart shows how an agricultural company spent £86 000 000 in one year on machinery, spares and repairs.

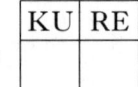

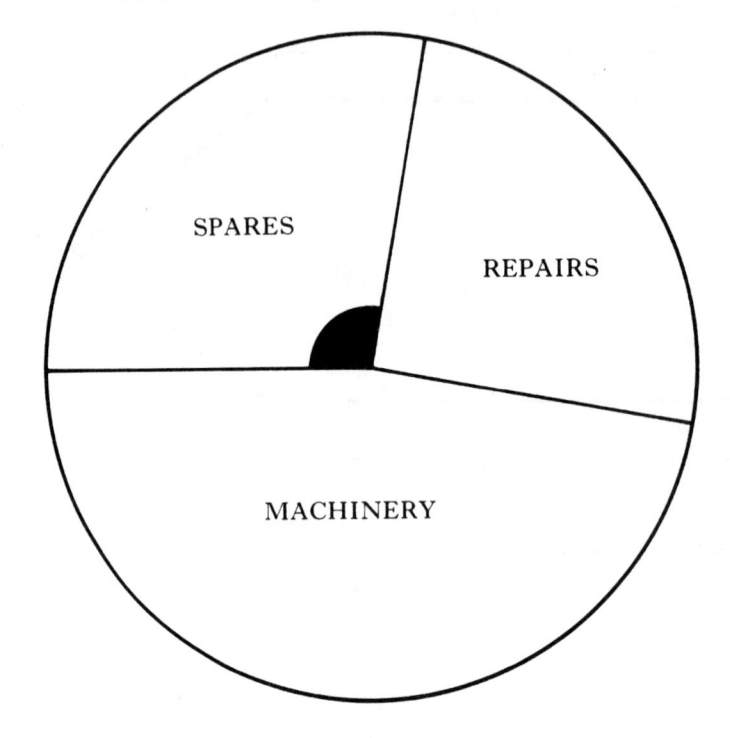

(a) Measure the size of the shaded angle.

(b) Calculate the amount of money spent on spares, giving your answer to the nearest million pounds.

8. A new regulation states that the gradient of all ramps into a building must be less than 0·26.

An existing ramp is 410 cm long and has a horizontal distance of 400 cm.

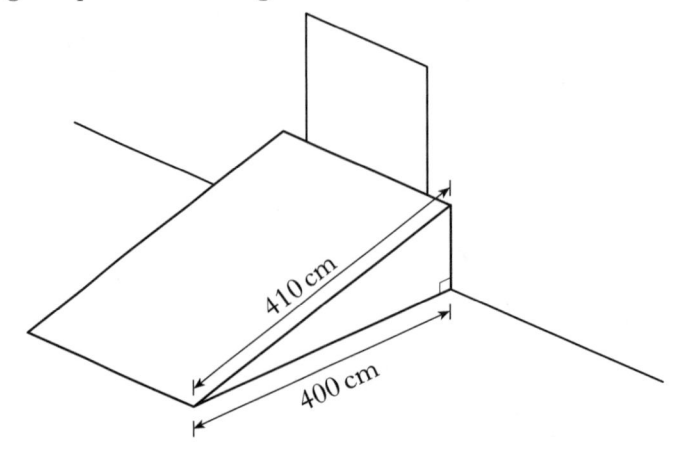

Does this ramp satisfy the new regulation?

Show all your working and give a reason for your answer.

9. A battery operated toy train travels on a circular track.

   The radius of the circle is 40 centimetres.

   It takes one minute for the train to travel 8 times round the track.

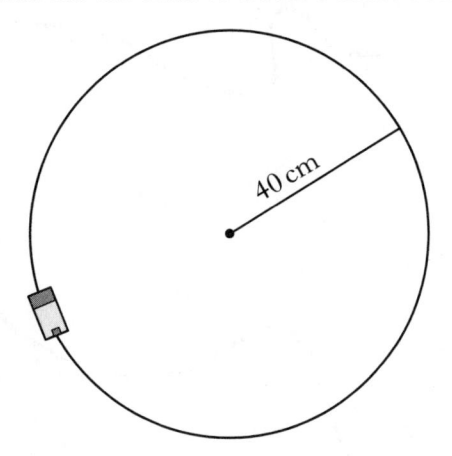

   (a) How far does the train travel in one minute?

   Give your answer to the nearest 10 centimetres.

   (b) Find the speed of the train in centimetres per second.

10. In a school hall, the stage is lit by a spotlight fixed to a wall.

    The spotlight is 4·35 metres up the wall and is set to shine on a spot on the stage 5·2 metres away from the wall, as shown in the diagram.

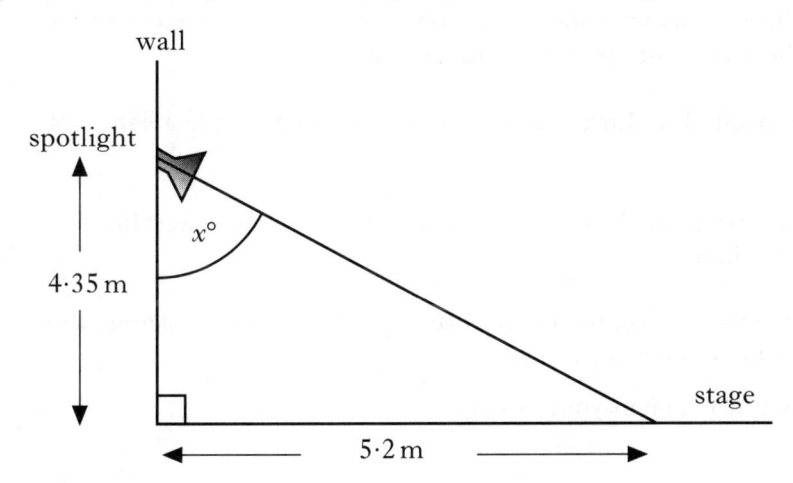

    Calculate the size of the angle marked $x°$.

    Do not use a scale drawing.

11. The diagram shows an island drawn to a scale of 1 centimetre to 20 kilometres.

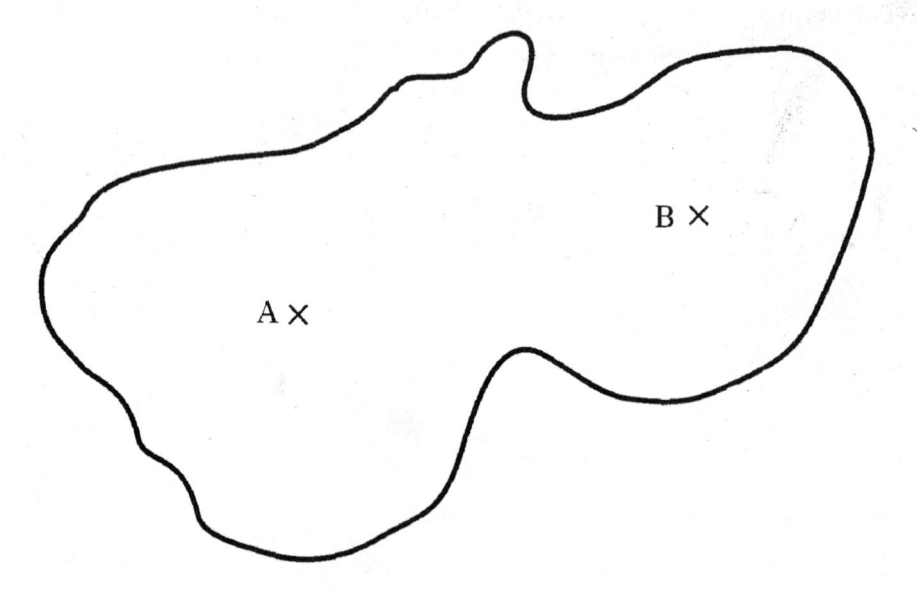

Scale: 1 cm to 20 km

The island has 2 radio transmitters.

The transmitter at A has a range of 80 kilometres, which means radio programmes can be heard up to 80 kilometres away from A.

The transmitter at B has a range of 60 kilometres.

(a) On the diagram above, show as accurately as you can the parts of the island where radio programmes can be heard.

It is planned to build a third transmitter on the island with a range of 20 kilometres.

(b) (i) Mark with an X on the diagram the best position for this transmitter.

(ii) Will this transmitter be sufficient to allow all the islanders to hear the radio programmes?

You must explain your answer.

12. Water is stored in a tank.

When the water level falls to a certain depth, the tank is automatically refilled.

The graph below shows the depth of water in the tank during a period of 24 hours.

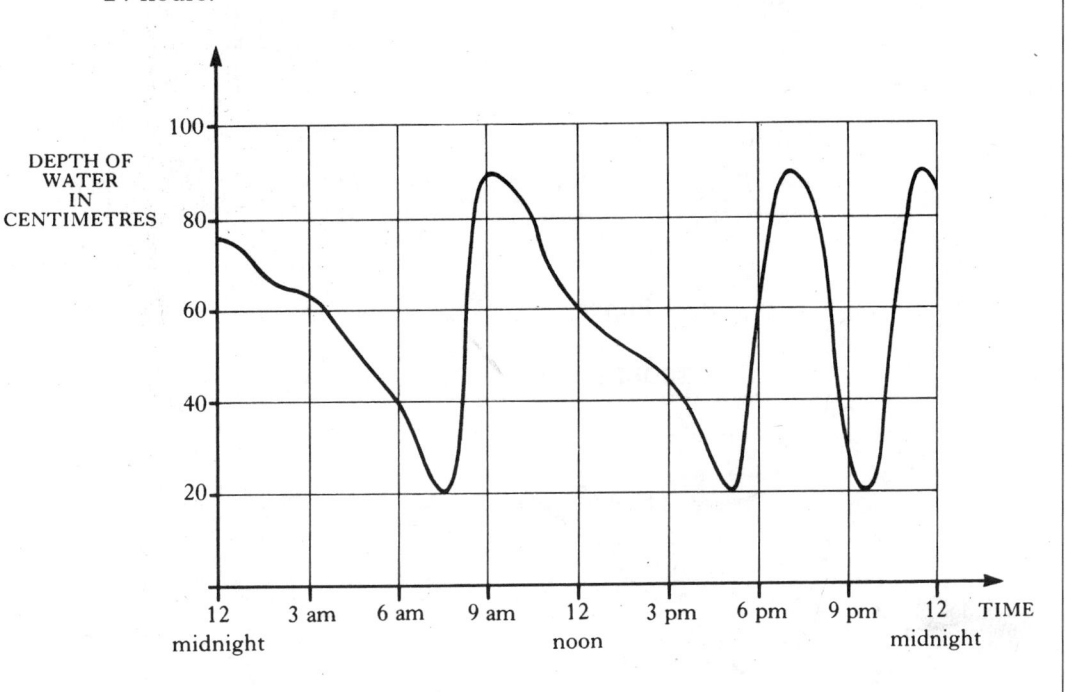

(a) How many times was the tank refilled during the 24 hours?

(b) What is the depth of the water when the tank has just been refilled?

(c) The water tank is in the shape of a cuboid of length 1·5 metres and breadth 1·2 metres.

How many litres of water are in the tank when it has just been refilled?

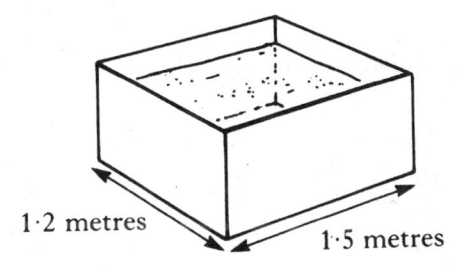

[END OF QUESTION PAPER]

ANSWERS — MODEL PAPER A
Paper 1

1. (a) £18.20 (b) 3·51 (c) 9·6 (d) 10·63   2. £108
3. (a) 2 330 000 (b) 2.33×10^6 4. (a) 11 °C (b) −9 °C
5. (a) [dot diagram] (b)

(s)	1	2	3	4	5		16
(d)	5	8	11	14	17		50

(c) $d = 3s + 2$

6. (a) 3 pm (b) Yes, 5.30 pm is earlier than 6 pm.
7. (a) $x = 9$ (b) $4(2a - 3b)$ 8. (a) Angle BPO = 22° (b) $x° = 46°$
9. 90 calls

Paper 2

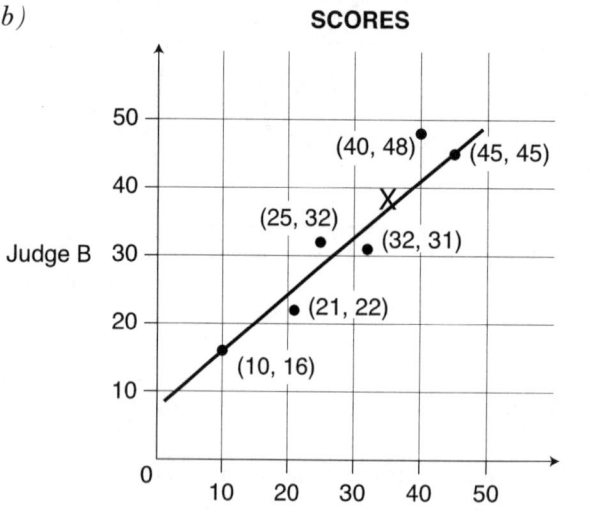

1. (a) & (b) **SCORES**   (c) 33

[Scatter graph: Judge B vs Judge A with points (10,16), (21,22), (25,32), (32,31), (40,48), (45,45) and best-fit line, X marked near (35, 38)]

2. (a) £149.50 (b) £99.67 (c) 7·53 years   3. Area = 644 cm²
4.

10	0	0	0	30
9	1	0	0	29
9	0	0	1	27
8	2	0	0	28
8	1	1	0	27
7	3	0	0	27

ANSWERS — Model Paper A

5. *(a)*

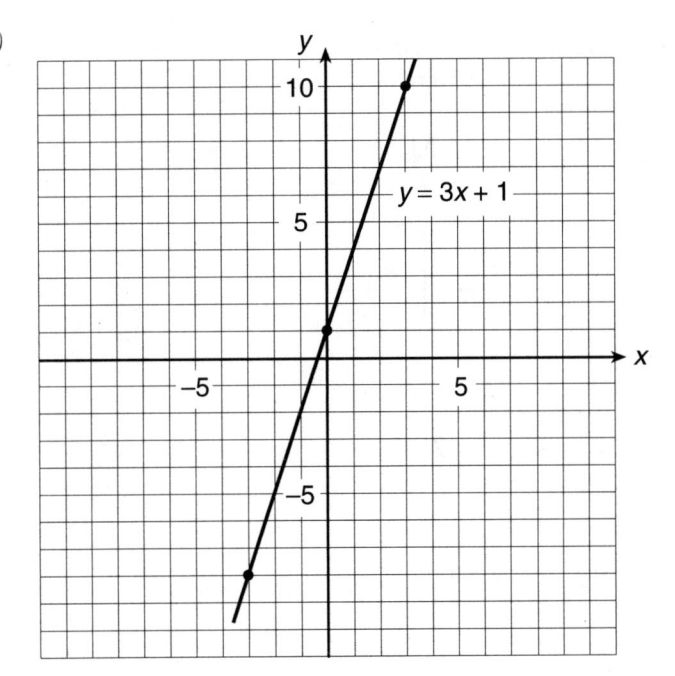

x	−3	0	3
y	−8	1	10

(b) [graph of $y = 3x + 1$]

6. *(a)* 112; mean = 12·1 *(b)* 4

7. 19·45 km

ANSWERS — Model Paper A

8. *(a)* Scale Drawing
1 cm : 5 km

(b) 15 cm : 75 km

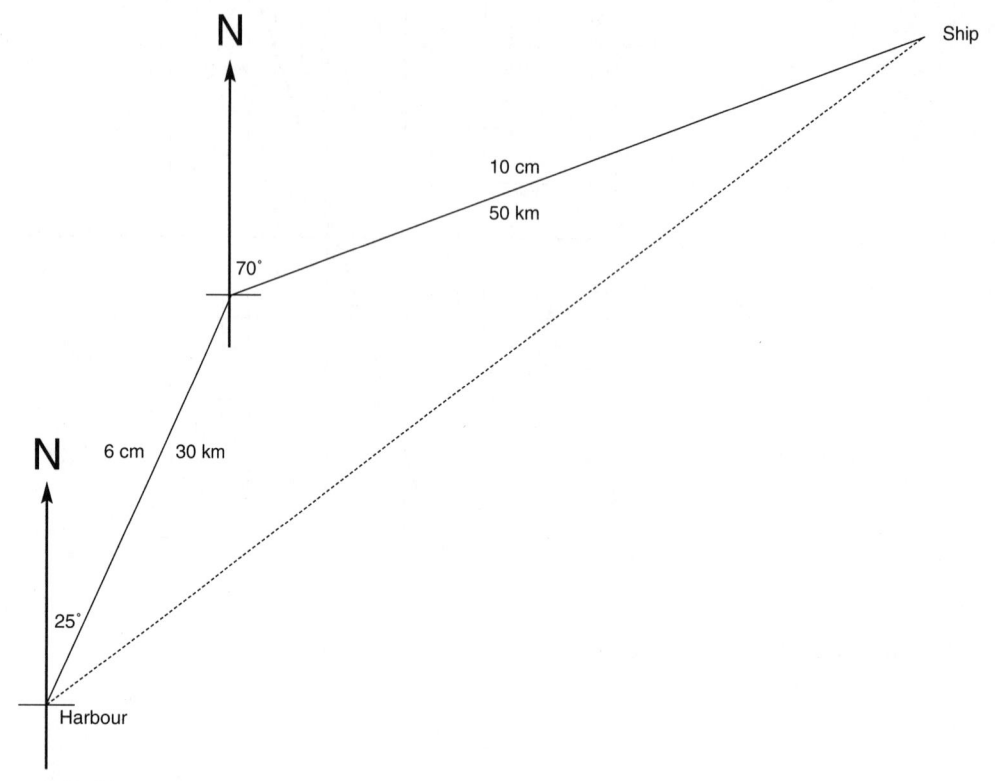

(Scale drawing: from Harbour, bearing 025° for 6 cm (30 km) to a point, then bearing 070° for 10 cm (50 km) to Ship; dotted line from Harbour to Ship.)

9. £58.50

10. $h \doteqdot 83{\cdot}3$ m

11. *(a)* 20 cm   *(b)* 8·4 cm

12. *(a)* 36 discs   *(b)* Area $\doteqdot 1482{\cdot}6$ cm^2

ANSWERS — MODEL PAPER B
Paper 1

1. (a) 30 m (b) 8·47 (c) 12·35 (d) 3·52
2. 0·000023   3. (a) 8 °C (b) 2 °C
4. (a) HEIGHT   (b) Darren is taller than Alexander
   (c) See diagram

   (c) • Claire
       • Darren
         • Alexander

   AGE

5. (a) Isosceles triangle (b) 40°
6. (a)

Number of sections (s)	1	2	3	4		10
Number of girders (g)	3	7	11	15		39

   (b) $g = 4s - 1$
7. (a) $14a - 15$ (b) $x = \dfrac{8}{3}$ 8. 44
9. $\dfrac{1}{5}$

Paper 2

1. (a) 246 km (b) 1 hour 49 mins (c) 135 km / h
2. (a) 2 (b) 48 (c) 32
3. (a) £350 (b) £16.25
4. (a) [graph showing A(−8, −3) and B(4, 6)]   (b) $\dfrac{3}{4}$

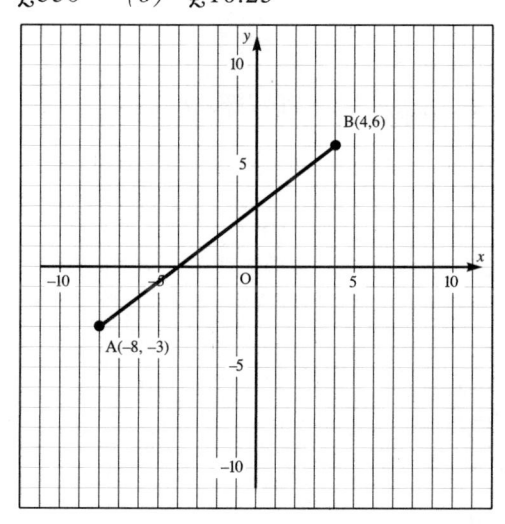

5. −2 °C

ANSWERS — Model Paper B

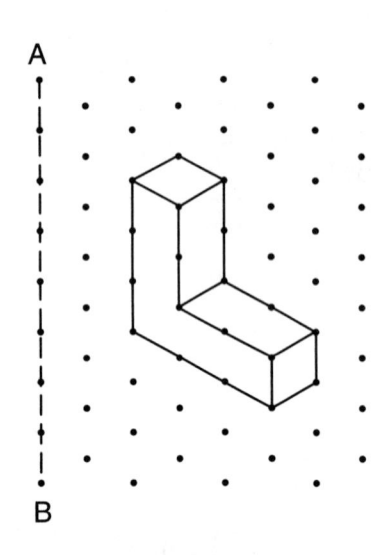

6. [isometric drawing of L-shaped solid on dotty paper, with vertical axis labelled A at top and B at bottom]

7. 212 cm

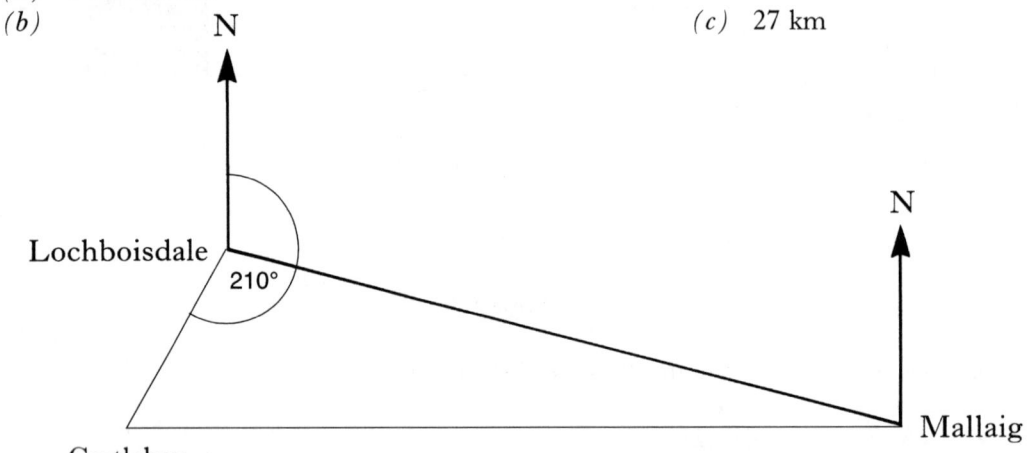

8. (a) 1 : 1 000 000
(b) [diagram showing bearing of 210° at Lochboisdale, with Castlebay and Mallaig marked]
(c) 27 km

9. Yes, 71° < A < 76°

10. (a) At £1.623 per litre Coverite is the cheapest (b) Tuffcote

11.

Number of Pack A	Number of Pack B	Number of Pack C
	1	2
		3
	2	1
1		2
	3	
1	1	1

12. (a) $V \doteqdot 501$ cm^3 (b) $L \doteqdot 11 \cdot 9$ cm

ANSWERS — MODEL PAPER C
Paper 1

1. (a) £225   (b) 2·767   (c) 3·9   (d) 9·58
2. (a) 15 hrs 36 mins   (b) Winter. In winter, darkness falls in the afternoon.
3. (a) £1·00   (b) 50p   (c) £7·00
4. (a)   (b) See diagram, point (1, 5)

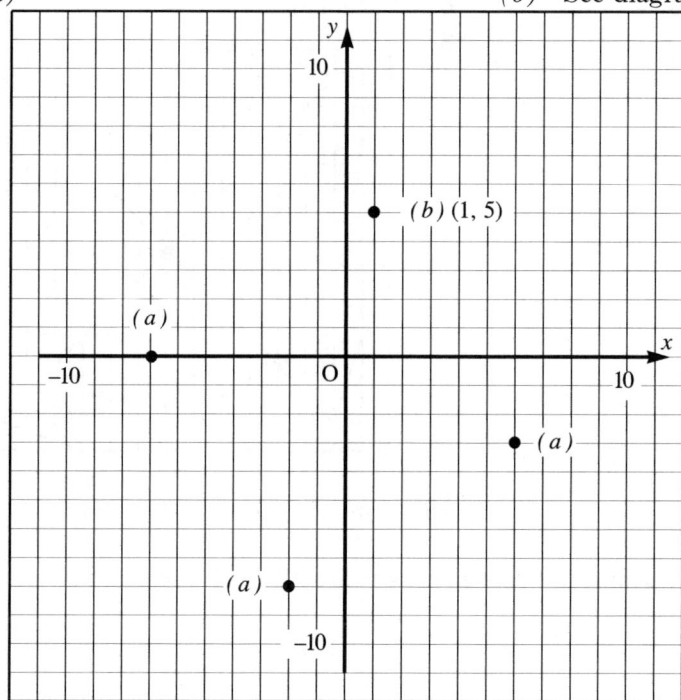

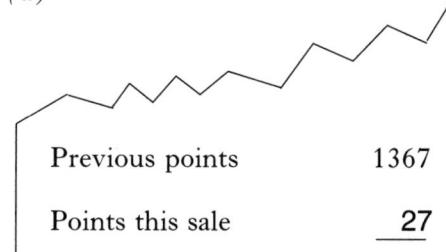

5. (a)   (b) £635

Previous points   1367
Points this sale   27
Total points   1394

6. (a) $x < 6$ (b) $5(3 - 2x)$ 7. 3·75 m   8. 40 mins

Paper 2

1. 382 400 lire   2.   12.75
                      124.32
                       32.94
                       29.75
                     £199.76

3. (a) (i) 7·4   (ii) 6
   (b) $\dfrac{2}{15}$

ANSWERS — Model Paper C

4. (a)

Number of Squares (N)	1	2	3	4	5	6
Number of Rods (R)	4	6	8	10	12	14

(b) $R = 2N + 2$ (c) 20 squares and 42 rods

5. (a) £56   (b) £2.50   **6.** 172·8 cm

7.
```
3 | 1 7 8 9
4 | 0 0 2 4 5 7 7 9
5 | 0 3 4 5 5
6 | 1 3
7 | 9
```
Key: 3 / 1 means 31

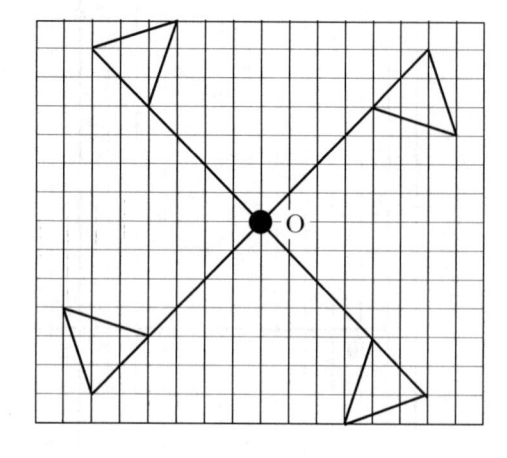

8.

9. Distance ≑ 10·3 km   **10.** (a) 5·6 cm   (b) 2·8 km
11. 23·6°
12. When data is plotted on a graph it forms a straight line through the origin.
13. 11 250 000 mm^3

ANSWERS — MODEL PAPER D

Paper 1

1. *(a)* 2106 *(b)* −35 *(c)* 816 *(d)* 0·615

2.
Time interval	Change in depth
Noon to 3 pm	up 43 metres
3 pm to 6 pm	Down 11 metres
6 pm to 9 pm	Up 28 metres
9 pm to midnight	Down 23 metres

3. *(a)* 56 miles
   (b) £30.80
   (c) £2394.40

4.

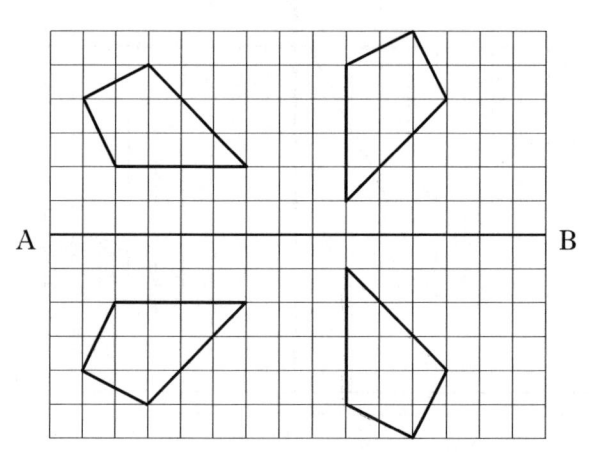

5. 10 hrs 15 mins
6. *(a)* $y < 3$
   (b) $3(5w + 2st)$
7. *(a)* 90°
   (b) 30°

8. 2 5 9 6
   2 6 5 9
   2 6 9 5
   2 9 5 6
   2 9 6 5

9. $\frac{1}{4}$

Paper 2

1. *(a)* £45 *(b)* Greece
2. *(a)* £4.00 *(b)* 3·7%
3. *(a)* −1 °C *(b)* −4 °C
4. Mortgages Direct better by £198.40
5. Yes, since 28 m > 27·6 m

ANSWERS — Model Paper D

6. (a)

x	−4	0	4
y	−7	1	9

(b) Graph of $y = 2x + 1$

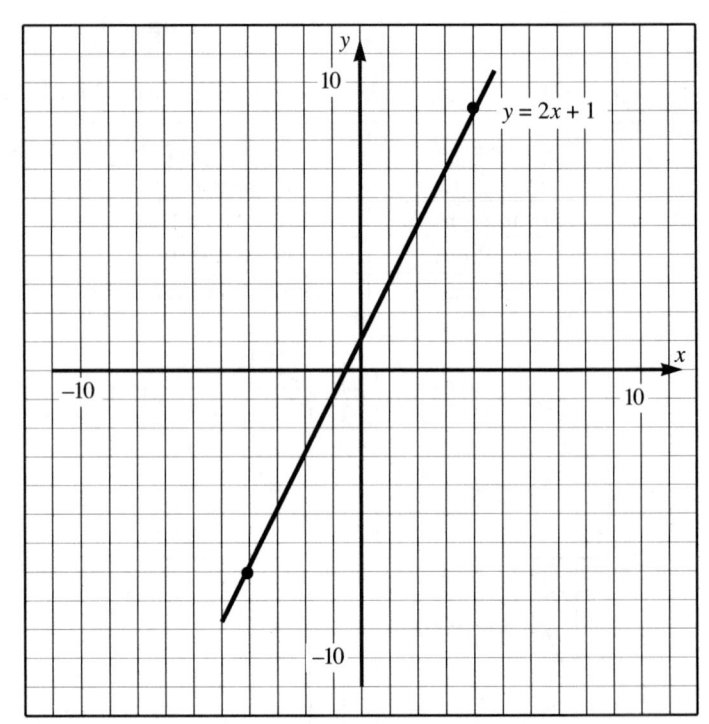

7.

Number of As	Number of Bs	Number of Cs	Number of Ds	Number of Points
7	–	–	1	21
5	3	–	–	21
6	1	1	–	21
6	2	–	–	22
7	–	1	–	22
7	1	–	–	23
8	–	–	–	24

8. 351 cm^3 **9.** 36 m

10. H = 4·90 m

11. (a) 50 packets (b) 66 cm (c) 7 boxes

12. (a) $r = 9300$ km (b) $S = 23\,400$ km / h

13. 110 mm

ANSWERS — MODEL PAPER E

Paper 1

1. (a) 1166 (b) 11·96 (c) −72 (d) 0·255
2. 190   3. 0·000 015 8
4. (a) Attendances are increasing
   (b) Attendances **rose** then **fell**   (c) Approx. 38 000
5. £149.00
6. (a) Let the twins age = x years   (b) Tamara is 16 years old
        $3x + 3 = 42$
7. (a) 3   (b)

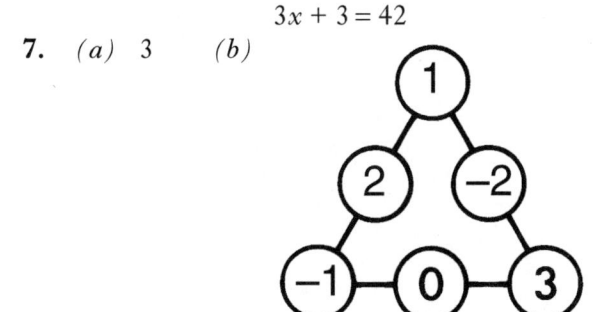

8. (a) R4 is 4 cm × 5 cm
   (b) Four R4 pieces can be cut from an R10 piece {R10 is 10 cm × 11 cm}

Paper 2

1. 6·8   2. £350
3. (a) 8.25 a.m.   (b) 3 km   (c) 4 k.p.h.
4. Yes, since 11 530 > 11 172. (70% of 15 960)
5. (a)

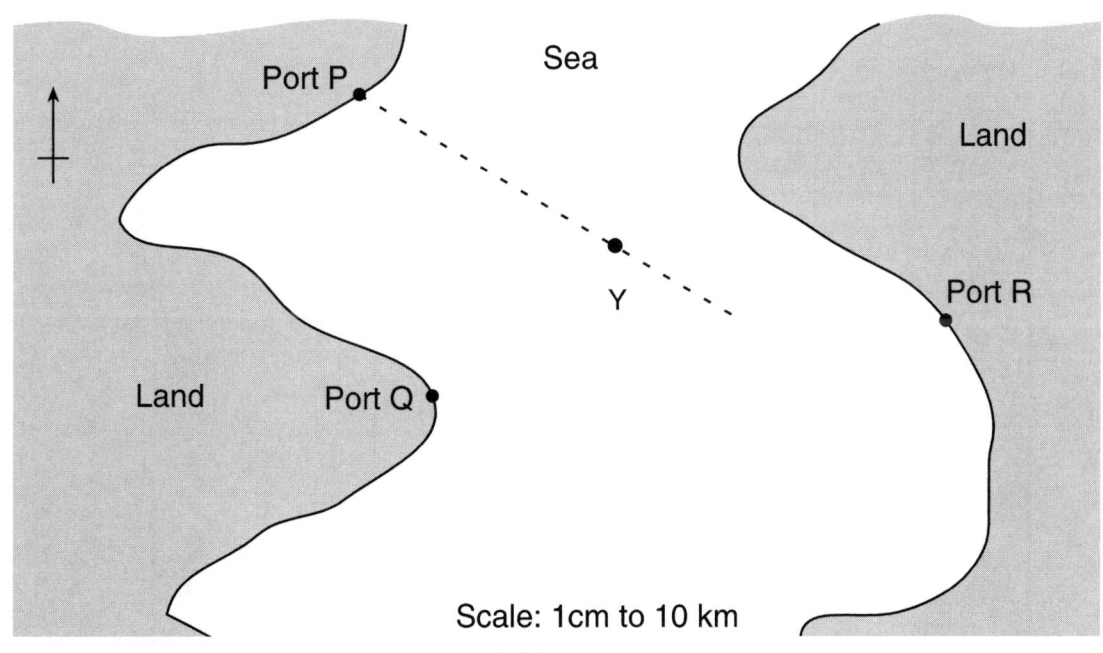

x	1	2	3	4	5	6
y	4		8	10	12	14

   (b) $y = 2x + 2$ (c) $a = 10$
6. R = 1·83
7. (a)

   (b) Port Q, nearest port   (c) 232°, distance 32 km

ANSWERS — Model Paper E

8. (a) 24 (b) $\frac{1}{49}$ (c) $\frac{25}{49}$

9. (a) 34·6 cm (b) 346 cm^2

10. 18 km

11. Yes, since 33·7° > 32°

12.

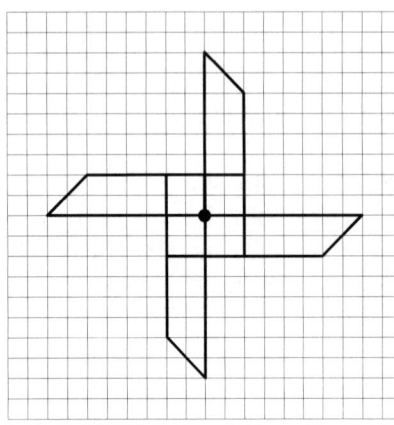

13. (a) 2229
      3336
      4443
      5550
    (b) 4443

ANSWERS — MODEL PAPER F

Paper 1

1. *(a)* 34 g *(b)* 11·48 *(c)* 214 *(d)* 8·09
2. 580
3. *(a)* 144 *(b)* $a = 7$ or -7
4. *(a)*

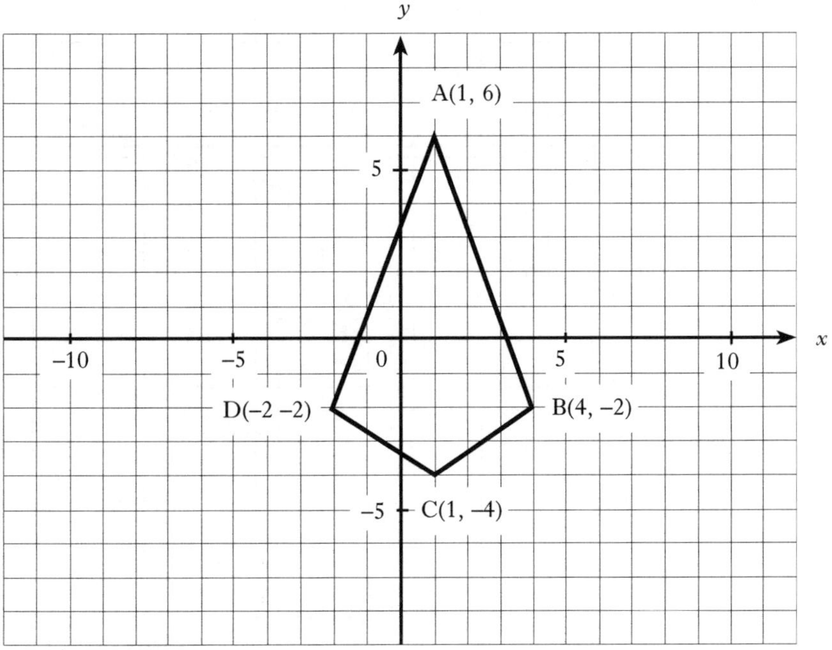

(b)

5. 60 cm^2
6. *(a)*

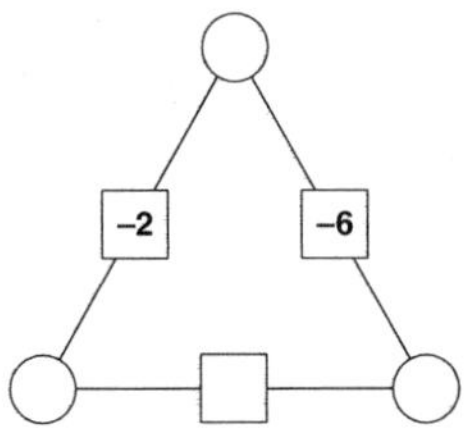

(b)

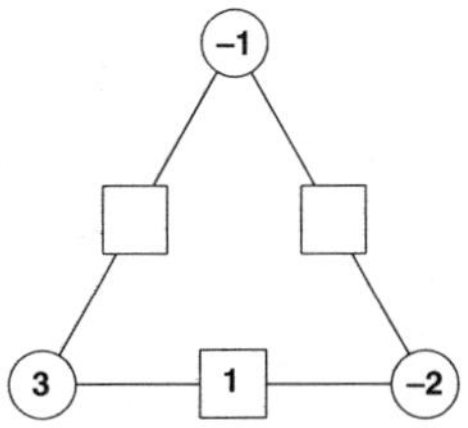

7. 1 pm
8. *(a)* $11x + 10y$ (b) $x = \frac{12}{5}$ or 2·4
9. *(a)* $y = (x - 1)(x - 4)(x - 7)$ *(b)* $y = (x + 2)(x - 2)(x - 4)$

Paper 2

1. *(a)* 51 *(b)* 31 *(c)* 51·7
2. £127.45
3. *(a)* 0·6 m^3 *(b)* 8
4. *(a)*

Number of miles	0	250	500	750	1000	1250	1500
"FREEDOM": cost in £	205	205	205	205	205	205	205
"ROVER": cost in £	145	160	175	190	205	220	235

ANSWERS — Model Paper F

(b) (i) & (ii)

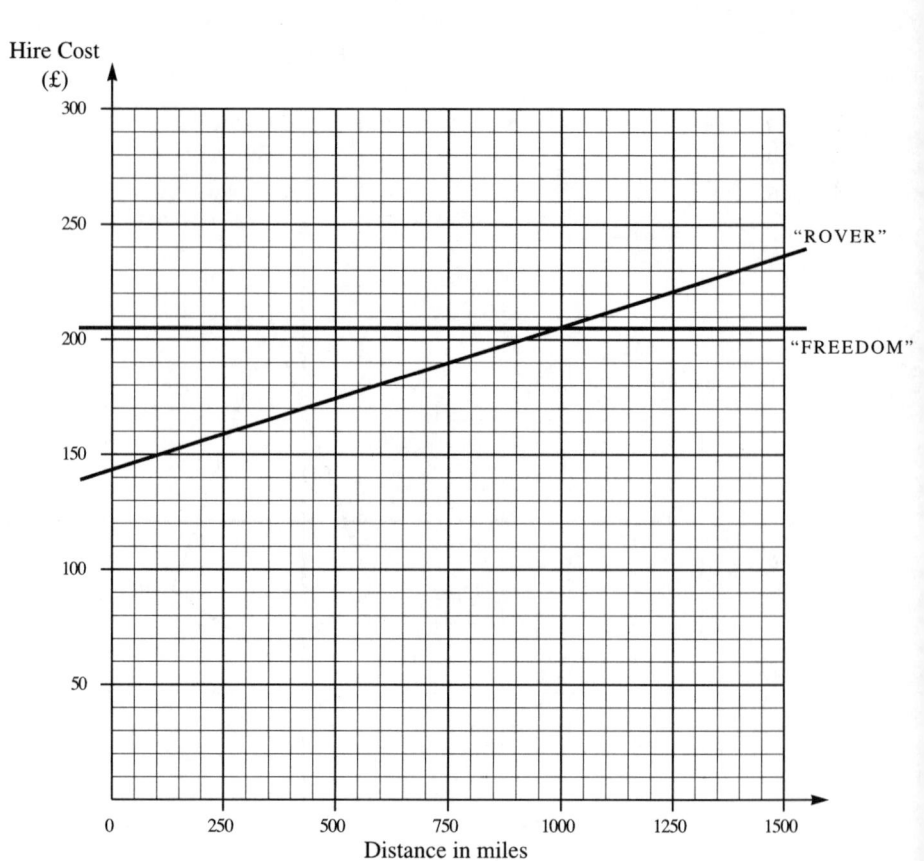

[Graph: Hire Cost (£) vs Distance in miles. "ROVER" line rising from about £140 at 0 miles to £240 at 1500 miles. "FREEDOM" horizontal line at £205.]

(c) Freedom scheme would be better. (It is £24 cheaper.)

5. 2100 cm^2 **6.** Yes, since 15% < 20% < 30%
7. (a) 100° (b) £24 million   **8.** Yes, it complies as 0·225 < 0·26
9. (a) 2010 cm (b) 33·5 cm per s   **10.** 50·1°
11. (a) On diagram {Scale drawing}
  (b) (i) On diagram
      (ii) Yes; since the whole island covered

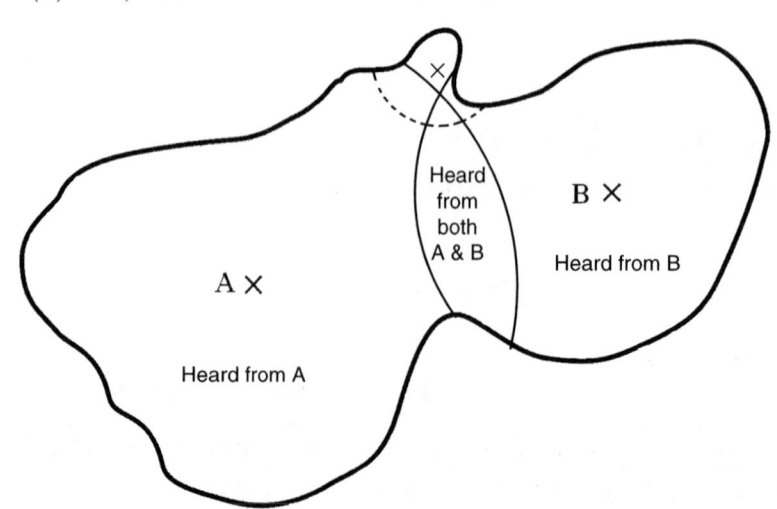

[Diagram of island showing point A × "Heard from A", point B × "Heard from B", overlap region "Heard from both A & B", with dashed arc near top marked ×]

12. (a) 3 times   (b) depth = 90 cm   (c) 1620 litres.

NOTES

NOTES

NOTES

NOTES